T0261525

**IoT-enabled Unobtrusive Surveillance
Systems for Smart Campus Safety**

IoT-enabled Unobtrusive Surveillance Systems for Smart Campus Safety

Theodoros Anagnostopoulos

IEEE PRESS

WILEY

Published by John Wiley & Sons, Inc., Hoboken, New Jersey.
Published simultaneously in Canada.

For general information on our other products and services or for technical support, please contact our Customer Care Department within the United States at (800) 762-2974, outside the United States at (317) 572-3993 or fax (317) 572-4002.

Wiley also publishes its books in a variety of electronic formats. Some content that appears in print may not be available in electronic formats. For more information about Wiley products, visit our web site at www.wiley.com.

Library of Congress Cataloging-in-Publication Data Applied for:

Hardback ISBN: 9781119903901

Cover Design: Wiley
Cover Image: © Quardia/Shutterstock

Set in 9.5/12.5pt STIXTwoText by Straive, Pondicherry, India

To Georgia, Vasileios, and Davidia for their priceless presence in my life.

Contents

Author Biography

 **THEODOROS ANAGNOSTOPOULOS** was born in Athens, Greece in 1976. He received the BEng degree from the University of West Attica, Greece, in 1997, the BSc and the MScIS degrees from the Athens University of Economics and Business, Greece, in 2001 and 2003, respectively. He received the PhD degree from the National and Kapodistrian University of Athens, Greece, in conjunction with the University of Geneva, Switzerland, in 2012. He also received the MScEd degree from the Hellenic Open University, Greece, in 2018. He was a postdoctoral researcher at the ITMO University, Russia, in 2015. He was a senior postdoctoral researcher at the University of Oulu, Finland, in 2016. He had been employed as a principal research scientist in smart cities at the Ordnance Survey: Great Britain's Mapping Authority, UK, in 2017. Currently, he holds a lecturer (teaching) academic position in computer science & engineering at the DigiT.DSS.Lab: Digital Transformation & Decision Support Systems in Business and Education Laboratory, at the University of West Attica, Greece. He holds, an associate academic position in artificial intelligence at the Essence: Pervasive & Distributed Intelligence Laboratory, at the University of Glasgow, UK. He also holds, an associated lecturer position in internet of things at the International Research Laboratory in Modern Communications Technologies and Applications in Economics and Finances, at the ITMO University, Russia. Dr. Theodoros Anagnostopoulos holds two patents in the research area of cognitive aware spatiotemporal authentication for smart and sustainable environments, in the USA and EU, where he is the inventor while intellectual properties are with Ordnance Survey: Great Britain's Mapping Authority, UK.

Preface

Smart campus is a living area of academics and students and can be considered as a miniature of a smart city (SC), also known as City 2.0. Living and studying in a smart campus is a challenging issue for thirsty young minds who want to form the future of human kind starting with research challenges at present to be able to lead the society in the future. Concretely, the concept of a smart campus extends the potentiality of an SC with regards to sustainable living of persons willing to research and explore the unexpected in the era of Industry 4.0. However, in such environments of human activity, it is possible that risks are emerged and should be mitigated. For example, malicious third-party entities might wish to cause inefficiencies in the physical infrastructure of the smart campus or even cause severe harm to individuals. To overcome such negative side effects, it is possible to apply a surveillance system to ensure physical safety of the personnel and the university campus infrastructure. The problem with surveillance systems is that humans do not wish to be monitored, thus such kind of systems are not actually used in practice. To overcome such an inefficiency, it is proposed that monitoring is performed unobtrusively, which means that surveillance systems respect user personality and protect fundamental human rights, such as privacy concerns, as defined by the general data protection regulation (GDPR) security policy making. In addition, it is given the option to campus users to negotiate their degree of free will to interact with certain services of the system, thus defining by their own the engagement they wish with the proposed system.

Specifically, what is fundamental in current research is the human factor as an unobtrusive surveillance system's adoption parameter for smart campus safety. The ability of a person to accept or decline safety services provided by such a system depends on the personal benefit of adopting an unobtrusive surveillance system in the workplace. An ethical dilemma is emerged by the incorporation of such a system in smart campus, which is the benefit of safety that the user deserves in comparison to the privacy data sacrifice the user is intended to accept. In plain words, the more the system penetrates human privacy space, the more the security services are provided to the user and vice versa. However, the user should be able to express the degree of free will, which will dictate the engagement the user accepts to provide for an unobtrusive system adoption. Lesson learnt in this research is that the center of an unobtrusive surveillance system in a smart campus is human population and specifically every unique human being with their free personality, which differentiates one specific individual from another in the same spatiotemporal university campus context. No system should be applied to users if they do not wish to be monitored by any system even if they risk their safety in the smart campus. What is proposed is that every single user is free to decide the degree the system will affect personal safety. So, it holds that the system should provide a scalable engagement to users' personality from no service provided, thus no surveillance service is activated, up to full surveillance provided, thus high-quality protection is applied to the affirmative user.

Athens   *Theodoros Anagnostopoulos*

1

Introduction

Smart cities (SC), also known as Cities 2.0, are embodiments of urban living in the digital age [1]. In the coming years, suburban and rural citizens are expected to move toward urban areas, forming a vast concentration of population in the inner city. It is anticipated that emerging paradigms such as Industry 4.0 will support the new needs of cities. A key component is the incorporation of the Internet of Things (IoT) paradigm as the backbone of society. IoT-enabled services will produce a vast amount of data that can be used to support and optimize critical infrastructure and provide new insights and advances. However, the majority of these data will be sensitive and should be treated unobtrusively not to harm freedom and individual privacy [2]. The challenge today is to understand how to build and deploy massively interconnected systems such that they are both effective and trustworthy. An academic research and industrial innovation area for learning a significant concept of safety systems is the application of surveillance mechanisms in smart campuses. A college or university campus is a scaled-down version of a city, which contains a somewhat closed community that is large enough to experience many of the technological, social, and human issues at a city scale [3]. In this study, a thorough and systematic survey on surveillance in smart campus systems is performed. This book is motivated by the lack of research that seeks to characterize the state of the art on smart campus surveillance.

Against this backdrop, the book surveys IoT-based surveillance systems in smart campuses, as these environments, although similar to smart cities, have some unique requirements that call for additional security and privacy measures. The present book proposes a survey, which was carried out on 44 systems that were deployed for campus safety. The author developed a taxonomy for these systems along with a scoring model for each one of them. The functionality of the surveyed systems was sized up against five dimensions: (1) physical infrastructure, (2) enabling technologies,

IoT-enabled Unobtrusive Surveillance Systems for Smart Campus Safety,
First Edition. Theodoros Anagnostopoulos.
© 2023 The Institute of Electrical and Electronics Engineers, Inc.
Published 2023 by John Wiley & Sons, Inc.

(3) software analytics, (4) system security, and (5) research methodology. The set of weights provided in the taxonomy enables a robust comparative assessment and classification model of state-of-the-art systems. Furthermore, the proposed method facilitates the extraction of valuable conclusions and inferences and gives insights and directions toward required services offered by a surveillance system of a smart campus. In addition, the survey brings forth a set of research efforts for the development of future surveillance systems specific to smart campuses [4]. Moreover, benefits of adopting an unobtrusive surveillance system in smart campus are analyzed. Concretely, special focus is given to the ethical dilemma of adopting such a system, while the degree of user's free will engagement with unobtrusive surveillance systems is exploited.

The contributions of this book in the areas of unobtrusive monitoring safety systems are as follows.

1.1 Smart Cities Dimensions and Risks

A definition of smart cities is provided as a living environment of academic inhabitants, which maximizes research and innovation outcomes. Consequently, analyses of the six fundamental dimensions of smart cities are performed, which are (1) smart economy, (2) smart governance, (3) smart living, (4) smart mobility, (5) smart people, and (6) smart environment. Each dimension is analyzed in detail and provided examples explain how each dimension affects green and sustainable physical infrastructure. In addition, there are exploited risks that arose in smart cities due to certain human malevolent behavior by using harmful contemporary technological advancements. These risks are divided in two major categories, regarding technology involvement to malicious behavior, which are technical and nontechnical risks. Subsequently, certain solutions to face smart cities' risks are proposed to mitigate malevolent behavior. Next topic of the study is the transition beyond the smart cities' concept to more compact systems, which are easily managed. Such systems could be the case of smart campuses.

1.2 Smart Campuses Components

Smart campuses focus on the potentiality assessment of existing systems beyond the smart city. Specifically, university campuses are living areas where efficient development and upgrade of software applications are performed. Such progress is supported by the adoption of cloud storage, 5G and 6G networking technology as well as edge AI, data science, and deep learning analyses capabilities. In addition, IoT devices produce online and real-time dynamic data sources, which are used to input intelligent systems and make early warnings and predictions of certain integrated application domains. To understand the operation background of a living smart campus, it is considered significant to separate five fundamental components, which describe university campus interoperability within both physical and digital worlds. Specifically, smart components are categorized as (1) smart grid, (2) smart community services, (3) smart management, (4) smart propagation services, and (5) smart prosperity. These components are derived from certain perspective of smart campus activity, such as social, environmental, and economic sustainability development processes. At this point, there is a transition from smart campus components and environment toward the adoption of a safe smart campus unobtrusive surveillance system to provide safety and privacy assurance to smart campus inhabitants.

1.3 Smart Campuses Unobtrusive Surveillance Systems

In this book, the concept of unobtrusive surveillance systems is defined as safety parameters in smart campus sustainable environment. Such concept is based on the five unique dimensions of the proposed taxonomy, which are also defined, namely (1) physical infrastructure, (2) enabling technologies, (3) software analytics, (4) system security, and (5) research methodology. These unique unobtrusive smart campus dimensions are used to deeply analyze the selected systems and exploit their potentiality in the area of smart campus safety. In addition, a taxonomy process is proposed that includes certain taxonomy components to assess the efficiency of the examined safety systems. Concretely, such taxonomy is based on the aforementioned defined five unobtrusive surveillance systems' dimensions, while it incorporates a weighted scoring system, which is specifically used for the classification and further assessment of the optimal quality of the adopted surveillance systems analyzed in this book.

1.4 Smart Campus Safety Systems Survey

Several university campus safety systems are analyzed extensively and surveyed based on certain group dimensions. The survey involves 42 papers and 2 patents, covering all the dimensions of the proposed taxonomy. Such dimensions are designed accordingly to provide an in-depth exploitation of the potentiality of each surveyed system. Smart campus safety is examined by certain groups of interest containing unobtrusive surveillance systems that focus on (1) systems not classified; (2) public spaces and smart parking; (3) smart buildings, smart labs, public spaces, and smart lighting; (4) public spaces and smart traffic lights; (5) smart buildings and smart classes; (6) smart buildings, public spaces, smart lighting, and smart traffic lights; (7) smart buildings and smart labs; (8) smart buildings and public spaces; (9) smart campus ambient intelligence and user context; and (10) smart campus low-power wide area networks and technology.

1.5 Smart Campuses Comparative Assessment

Smart campus systems' strengths and weaknesses are the basis of the analysis that is performed to define a concrete as well as equal comparative assessment. Such assessment aims to present each system's potentiality to face a malevolent behavior in smart campuses. Proposed systems' comparison is based on exploiting the potentiality of the certain five unique dimensions adopted by the proposed taxonomy during the performed safety systems' survey.

1.6 Smart Campus Systems Classification

While comparative assessment presents the efficiency of each surveyed system adopted, classification process separates the results to provide added value to observed outcomes. Concretely, classification is based on the adopted weighted scoring system. Intuitively, each system is classified in one of three proposed classes to provide an outcome of the surveyed monitoring systems. The first class contains the contemporary advanced surveillance systems, while the optimal system that is part of the first class will be addressed.

1.7 Smart Campus Safety: A System Architecture

Optimal smart campus safety is presented in this section to assess its potentiality. Concretely, smart campus safety system is disused, which incorporates an unobtrusive surveillance system with a compact architecture. Such system architecture presents the key components of the surveillance system, which is based on each campus users' spatiotemporal fingerprint. This fingerprint is unique for each university campus user, where the method of its creation and processing to provide unobtrusive monitoring and safety by malevolent individuals is presented. Such fingerprint is based on spatial and temporal data of each user captured during their daily activity in the smart campus. Surveillance mechanisms embedded in the campus infrastructure to feed the spatiotemporal fingerprint include a variety of components, such as closed-circuit television (CCTV) camera networks, microphone networks, automated teller machine (ATM) networks, connected and autonomous vehicle (CAV) networks, unmanned aerial vehicle (UAV) networks, surveillance humanoid robot networks for systems' safety, as well as other emerging monitoring devices.

An authorization system is also proposed, which exploits spatiotemporal fingerprint authentication to provide an early warning and prediction when an unauthorized individual tries to enter the system without adequate permission. Concretely, the system is able to distinguish between a certain, not authorized, malevolent individual who wish to harm the system and a smart campus user who might seem as a malicious user but actually needs to invoke system's data updating processes to update their spatiotemporal fingerprint. In the latter case, the user is part of the system, but there is a need to enable system's processes to be re-recognized by the system access module to be able to gain access in a certain area and/or asset of the campus. Such a university campus system is proposed to be used for designing future surveillance systems aiming at smart campuses' safety.

1.8 Human Factor as an Unobtrusive Surveillance System's Adoption Parameter for Smart Campus Safety

On acceptance of an unobtrusive surveillance system by university campus population, human factor is a key point where it should be treated gently. This is because every technical system is able to be adopted by human population only if it respects fundamental human rights, such as individual's freedom to adopt a proposed technology or not. Concretely, proposed system deals with the ethical dilemma of adopting an unobtrusive surveillance system based on certain issues to be considered, such as (1) privacy, (2) ethical, and (3) social implications of a monitoring smart campus system. Intuitively, university campus actors should be provided the option to evaluate their degree of free will engagement and negotiation with the proposed unobtrusive system. Monitoring system provides end users the feasibility to share their private data with the system in the degree they wish to acquire proposed system's safety services.

1.9 Smart Campus Surveillance Systems Future Trends and Directions

The book concludes by summarizing the analytical survey performed that focused on smart campus as a socially acceptable solution, since contemporary universities are open to experiment with emerging management regulations, as well as to try applying intuitively new safety solutions. Specifically, there are some real implications, which make these systems acceptable by the scientific community, such as the prevention and repression of delinquent behavior as well as studying the motivation and the development behind this behavior. The findings in this research focus on important aspects in future research directions, such as to verify the impact of scientific invention in the area of IoT-enabled smart campus monitoring systems toward an industrial innovation for the well-being of humans.

The rest of the book is structured as follows. Chapter 2 presents the fundamental sociotechnical paradigm of future habitation, which is the concept of a smart city. Chapter 3 focuses on smart campus as an area of human engagement, which is considered as a miniature of smart city. Chapter 4 specifies the adoption of unobtrusive surveillance systems by smart campus. Chapter 5 performs survey analyses to state-of-the-art systems for smart campus safety. Chapter 6 conducts comparative assessment on the surveyed systems. Chapter 7 performs classification of the analyzed systems and proposes optimal solutions based on the assessment of the systems. Chapter 8 examines a case study of the optimal spatiotemporal authentication unobtrusive surveillance system architecture for smart campus safety. Chapter 9 describes human factor as an unobtrusive surveillance system's adoption parameter for smart campus safety. Chapter 10 finally concludes the findings of the book and discusses smart campus surveillance systems' future trends and directions.

2

Smart City

The concept of smart cities' (SCs) is analyzed and designed in different regions worldwide. There is an actual need for exploitation of information and communications technology (ICT) potentiality in SCs. Different dimensions of human activity should be considered to the development of SC planning and implementation [5]. This inherent complexity exists within each dimension of the city. Such complexity needs treatment based on incorporated technologies and their integration, which brings the risk uncertainty parameter as part of the implementation phase of the SC concept. In case these risks are not effectively understood and faced, it is possible they could create critical issues in terms of citizens' privacy and security, which might have severe effects in the SCs' functionality. In this chapter, dimensions are identified, available technologies are addressed, technical and nontechnical risks are presented, and risk management to mitigate SCs' risks are discussed to support SCs implementation.

2.1 Smart Cities Dimensions

Smart cities are the future of human habitation since 67% of human population will live in such cities by 2050. Certain infrastructure should be adopted to ensure a viable green and sustainable ecosystem to citizens. Living in an SC is challenging since new problems have emerged and they infrastructure, there are certain risks need to be faced by the local authorities, such as fresh water provision, traffic handling in rush hours during the day to provide green transportation, and smart home architectural design to provide citizens a promising well-being. SCs are composed by six fundamental dimensions, which are (1) smart economy, (2) smart governance, (3) smart living, (4) smart mobility, (5) smart people, and (6) smart

IoT-enabled Unobtrusive Surveillance Systems for Smart Campus Safety, First Edition. Theodoros Anagnostopoulos.
© 2023 The Institute of Electrical and Electronics Engineers, Inc.
Published 2023 by John Wiley & Sons, Inc.

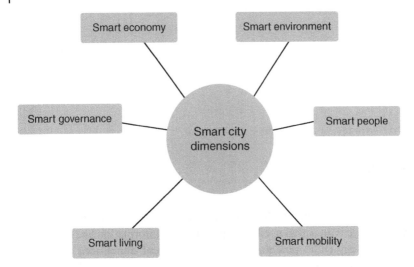

Figure 2.1 Smart city dimensions.

environment [6]. Fulfillment of all SC dimensions assures the quality of living in such a city. It holds that a successful city should have high level of engagement and social activity with the SC dimensions. In addition, since SCs are a living environment, which includes the collaboration of citizens and technical infrastructure, there are certain risks that need to be addressed. Such risks are either technical or nontechnical. To face different kind of risks, certain risk analysis and assessment tools should be considered by the SC management personnel. SC dimensions are presented in Figure 2.1.

2.1.1 Smart Economy

Smart economy is well aligned with legislation and policies relevant to business innovation and industrial creativity. Economic innovation engages scientific research in upcoming technological progress as well as enables sustainability toward a green ecosystem. Smart economy might conceive certain areas of ICT as well as industrial innovation and competitiveness as part of the contemporary economic trends aiming for the efficient use of socially responsible resources. Conventional theories in the field of economic research imply that smart economy in the context of SC habitation promotes at-hand experience and valuable knowledge, which is based on state-of-the-art academic innovation [7]. Such innovation is applied horizontally in many research areas of human activity including science, industry, social cultural heritage, logistics, and planning, as well as business research and development. There are many applications and directions of smart economy activities within SC development. Every research direction has its unique economic characteristics well aligned with upcoming challenges and proposed solutions. Emerging areas of smart economy dimension for SCs' sustainability are extended to certain application domains, such as (1) entrepreneurship and innovation, (2) productivity and employment, and (3) international embeddedness. These areas are promising in enabling citizen well-being in SCs. This in fact holds because such domains provide the pillar of smart economy ongoing progress, which results in every single citizen's daily quality of life and enhanced social activity.

2.1.2 Smart Governance

Smart governance refers to the study of SC structural dimensions along with challenges and proposed solutions provided to support the legal authorities of the city. A key concept of smart governance is the sufficient contribution in decision-making processes aiming to provide solutions to everyday problems that might arise in the sustainable environment. Certain SC digital infrastructures, such as social services and transparent governance, should be provided to citizens to assess the effectiveness level of municipality's smart governance. Local authorities are responsible to apply specific policies and strategies adding the value of citizens' well-being. It is obvious that smart governance is the outcome of decent collaboration between citizens, local authorities, and administrative institutions to provide efficient services to human population [8]. Such outcomes can further provide maximal sociotechnical benefits to SC infrastructure by enabling reliability, efficiency, and effectiveness of citizens' assistance, which in turn focus to the integration of public, private, and civil operations. In addition, technical governance is a critical parameter of smart governance because it is able to provide SC state-of-the-art solutions due to sustainable and technological maturity. In this research, smart governance is further divided to certain subdomains, such as (1) non-ICT infrastructure, (2) online services, and (3) open governance. These domains address all SC services provided to citizens while assuring the ability of the city to research and innovate in the area of governance. Actually, governance is considered the basic building block of all collective efforts incorporated to provide effective interactions with all stakeholders in SCs. Future of smart governance should be interactive with the actors of the city to promote research invention and open industrial innovation. This kind of social interaction could be enhanced with the proliferation of e-governance, which might progress in the direction of building social engagement and transparency in municipality decision-making processes. E-governance is possible to be applied in SC policies with the advancements in the areas of 5G and 6G technologies, as well as the optimizations performed in present in the research field of edge artificial intelligence (AI) and Internet of Things (IoT). Cloud-based architecture as well as big data analytics are able to provide the technical test bed, which is fundamental to evaluate e-governance participation engagement as well as effective validation of information sharing and smart governance in further collaboration.

2.1.3 Smart Living

Smart living is the concept of considering the development and preservation of certain elements, such as nature green ecosystem quality, economic growth, and human capital management. Smart buildings, smart public spaces, society's education level, and health care infrastructure are forming the notion of social context awareness as a principal parameter of smart living. Online real-time health care monitoring can save lives of elderly and impairs citizens. In addition, special care and medical support with IoT technology can assist medical professionals in health emergency situations, like the case of covid-19 pandemic. By another point of view, smart living could also be considered as the social result of smart economy is SCs. Specifically, the use of ICT aims to provide advanced services in the areas of digital networking, IoT-enabled smart public spaces, SC lighting, as well as autonomous and connected safety systems. Smart homes provide smart assistance to citizens' daily activities by exploiting user-generated private data, which should be protected under the general data protection regulation (GDPR) safety and privacy assurance legislation. Insight of SC's data sources emerges the need of transparency and open-data policies to provide high-quality services for users' smart living [9]. Toward these directions, standards and data specifications should be examined to enhance smart applications, which will be able to perform detection and management actions related with certain risk assessment methods. In addition, such challenging smart applications, which support quality of living in the SC, incorporate state-of-the-art available technologies including but not limited to data science, AI, machine learning, user profiling, cloud and edge storage and computing, as well as networking technologies and wireless sensor networks architectures. Smart living should exploit the potentiality of such technologies to provide quality of life the SC population.

2.1.4 Smart Mobility

Smart mobility focuses on intelligent transport systems (ITS) and IoT-based transportation infrastructure. Specifically, there are many open issues in the area of smart mobility including vehicle congestions in central roadways as well as long queues of traffic bottlenecks and significant time of arrival delays to reach certain destinations on time. Vehicle ride sharing systems and carpooling architectures could assist user movements and commuting in the SC. Real data are possible to be gathered by existing IoT infrastructure in the road network aiming in performing routing analytics [10]. Such analytics incorporate local knowledge gathered by edge AI technology to provide quality of service (QoS) to prospective travelers. Smart mobility policies are feasible in the SC ITS due to the exploitation connected and autonomous vehicles (CAV) potentiality. Such vehicles are characterized by high degree of traffic safety and movement efficiency in urban and rural transportation. In addition, IoT-enabled transportation architecture in urban and rural areas of the city would provide a safer integrated ITS for smart citizens' mobility. Moreover, smart mobility should be considered by multiple aspects of users' movement activity. Such activity promotes development of technical solutions and innovative technological advances in the areas of big data analytics, IoT, machine learning, and AI, as well as blockchain potentiality.

2.1.5 Smart People

Smart people is the SC dimension, which focuses on the social part of human habitation in smart cites. Such habitation involves human and social capital management and prosperity, as well as the interconnections between citizens' way of life either as individuals or as part of a group of people. Specifically, human capital focuses on the abilities and the proficiencies of an individual or a group of persons in the city, while social capital is divided as the quantity and quality of relations and reactions connecting social infrastructure and organizations. There is a need for high-quality human and social capital as part of the SC's industrial innovation and business productivity. In addition, smart living is well aligned with smart people dimension and human capital in SCs in different areas of human activity, such as higher education institutes of research including universities and living laboratories [11]. It is considered that smart campuses and living labs of universities as well as other higher educational and research institutes have the role of knowledge mediators. Such institutes are able to provide mentoring, support, and companionship services to young thirsty minds and other people wishing to become smart and intelligent. Certain key enabling technologies are used for reaching these goals, like edge AI, big data science, and IoT to develop and deploy smart applications for enhancing learning, knowledge sharing, and teaching. However, there arose challenging issues with respect to privacy and safety services' information shared with the people, which should be handled unobtrusively by the appropriate third parties of smart campuses. QoS is an essential aspect of smart education higher institutes, which engage students and citizens with the government processes by incorporating cutting edge technologies, such as IoT and edge computing. For example, an e-government website provides social services to SC population while allowing interaction of citizens with open and proactive public services available to all city's stakeholders.

2.1.6 Smart Environment

Smart environment is related to policies and actions toward a green ecosystem. Emerging issues include sufficient energy management, population control, smart grids, waste management and recycling, quality of air and fresh water, housing and facility management, care for green public spaces, as well as vehicle and industry emissions monitoring. Technology is considered as a collaborator to provide sustainable solutions, such as natural resources preservation and maintenance [12]. In addition, natural resources should be treated with sustainable methods to protect the environment, manage the existing resources, and reduce environmental pollution. Such methods contain but are not limited to smart energy grids, which are able to produce and consume green energy, as well as sustainable buildings development. IoT is an enabling technology, which supports smart environment by developing applications to assist sustainable ecosystems. Different types of sensors and actuators, such as radio frequency identification (RFID), chemical sensors, fire sensors, humidity sensors, pressure sensors, volume sensors, and weight sensors, are incorporated to manage the environment of the SC. Online real-time data collection and processing provides significant aid to SC decision-makers to optimize waste management recycling and further waste processing. Exploiting IoT and AI technology potentiality is able to provide accurate SC logistics and decision strategy to assist well-being and social activities of citizens.

2.2 Risks Related to Smart Cities

IoT and contemporary technology enable the concept of SCs as green ecosystems, where human population experiences different kind of services aiming for citizens' well-being. Such services include technical advancements in logistics, healthcare, transportation, education, economy, and environment controlled and assessed with the proliferation of smart devices [13]. Each of these services is automated by incorporating a plethora of technologies, which are controlled by certain human activity. In addition, human activity is relevant to available resources and budget to complete assigned tasks. The fact that development of SCs is prone to resource allocation and adequate budget increases the risks of certain aspects. Specifically, risks existing in SCs are grouped accordingly in two categories such as technical risks and nontechnical risks, which are analyzed subsequently.

2.2.1 Technical Risks

Technical risks are associated with technical advancements, mainly in the areas of IoT, big data analytics, and AI. Technical risks are referring to technology and contemporary implementation in SCs. Specifically, IoT technology is probe to cybersecurity. This is explained since connected IoT components, such as sensors and actuators, are developed in the SC infrastructure including health, transportation, as well as energy transmission. Proliferation of such devices exposes SC resource allocation vulnerability to active risks relevant to hacking and various malevolent behavior, such as cybercrime. In addition, cybersecurity expands in other areas except the main area of IoT sensors and actuators technology [14]. Such areas include wireless networks and SC portal inefficiencies. Privacy and security of citizens' personal data should also be considered by adopting intrusion detection and authentication systems to mitigate risks and address upcoming cybersecurity issues. AI is another area suffering from technical risks due to complex systems, which should be controlled effectively to face a possible compromise. Such risks might cause legal issues, which require certain verifications of compliance with the law regulation regarding fundamental human rights that need to be protected. AI systems are used extensively in the areas of energy, security, education, transport, health urban management, and sustainable environment to provide systems able to make predictions and preform early warning signaling. Security AI-based systems are able to perform early threat recognition including various treats, such as economic fraud, crime, fire detection, and accident proactive prediction. Blockchain technology studies risk issues related to contemporary solutions of security and privacy threats related to IoT components in the SC infrastructure. Such technology is based on a point-to-point distributed network architecture where a transaction is verified only when a registered node validates and stores it in a central ledger. This feature of blockchain technology enables the use of a network, which enhances data security within the IoT infrastructure. It is possible to manage security and privacy requirements by enabling events, which are initialized by several trusted IoT devices. In addition, blockchain technology can be used to assure transactions safety and privacy in areas like low productivity, data storage, and energy effectiveness.

2.2.2 Nontechnical Risks

Although SCs are an area of cutting-edge technology where several technical risks have emerged, there are also risks that could be characterized as nontechnical risks. Such nontechnical risks have side effects on the operation and the implementation of sustainable SCs. Specifically, risks are related to organizational and legal situations between public and private sectors in SCs. A detailed list of nontechnical risks includes governance, strategy, legal, and socioeconomic risks. Socioeconomic risks refer to the mindset of SC stakeholders as well as decision makers. Smart city research and innovation projects require certain budget, developed personnel, adequate technology advancements, and engagement of professionals, citizens, and decision-makers. Social risks refer to different actors, such as SC regulators, technology companies, customers, and energy service providers.

Such actors aim to perform better efficiency, cost control, and green ecosystem sustainability. In addition, public engagement has an impact on SC's ability to provide quality of life and social efficiency. Strategic risks emerge in SCs in case a strategic approach is not linked between ICT infrastructure research agenda and sustainability development [15]. The lack of this linkage leads to wastage of investments relevant to ICT development while concretely increasing socioeconomic and environmental concerns. In addition, SC management needs to collaborate with stakeholders to discuss strategic risks and opportunities in strategy formulation and further implementation. Legal and governance risks focus on SC projects in terms of socio-political niche with several risks associated with laws, rules, policies, social, and political forces. Approvals of SC projects raise legal concerns related to unobtrusive monitoring, stakeholder, and resource management, which are upcoming factors needed to be considered in SC governance. In addition, privacy and security concerns are possible to become prominent in case the legal system is not validated and updated to face the emerging issues of technology integration and dissemination of information. Legal technology and low enforcement should be developed in SCs, such as the incorporation of closed-circuit television (CCTV) systems, city coverage with wireless frequency, automated teller machines (ATM), e-payments, and digital transactions. Moreover, ethical standards should be posed by the SC municipality and governance authorities to assure citizens' data privacy, safety, and storage.

2.3 Mitigating Smart Cities Risks

Risk management in an SC includes undertaken technology choices, adopted strategies, cause of risks, observed responses, derived consequences, as well as contingency plans to mitigate risk ambiguity. However, such a concept in SCs is not addressed in great detail due to time limitations and financial constraints. Risk management is well aligned with project performance processes, which is achieved by managing and monitoring risk uncertainty factors on project objectives. Specifically, risk management incorporates certain strategies, which are crucial for the success of the SC project [16]. In addition, contemporary research is able to evaluate such strategies eliminating uncertainties by incorporating fuzzy weighted mean methodologies. Such methodologies are able to support decision-makers to choose an optimal strategy for their project. Risk analyses and risk assessment are two areas of risk management, which should be continuously performed to develop a risk response strategy able to face each SC dimension. However, it should be noted that each SC dimension should be treated independently. Risk analyses is based on certain actions applied to SC dimensions to assess emerging uncertainties, which might affect SC's further processes and sustainable operations. In addition, risk assessment is considered a vital parameter to overcome the upcoming management challenges in an SC's project. There are multiple risk assessment techniques, each of them applied in a specific SC dimension.

2.4 Systems Beyond Smart Cities

Living in SCs is challenging since the environment is enhanced with Industry 4.0 embodiments, such as CAV, unmanned aerial vehicles (UAV), and robot systems. Citizens should be able to live and prosper in such a heterogeneous green ecosystem. Certain risks have emerged in cases where public safety is challenged by actions of malicious entities (i.e. terrorist attacks) in different areas in the city. For example, a terrorist organization might cause harm by a bomb attack in a public building or a metro station. In this case, city needs security countermeasures to provide citizens a safe way of living. However, safety has the price of users' private data penetration by accepting an unobtrusive surveillance system for malevolent entities protection. In general, society is not ready yet to accept such a safety system since humans do not feel comfortable to live in such an environment. In addition, certain technical and nontechnical risks have emerged within the SC operation. Such risks should be mitigated by certain risk analyses and assessment tools to assure citizens' well-being. What is proposed in current study is to move focus from SC to smart campus, which is a miniature of SC. Smart campus contains young student population and would like to experiment with new ways of human interaction and future social living. This feature enables the experimentation with smart campus unobtrusive surveillance systems at present, while it prepares humanity for such a step in the next citizen generation.

3

Smart Campus

Smart campus is a system beyond the concept of smart city. Such campus is an emerging research area with many upcoming trends, which allows higher educational institutes to combine contemporary technologies with physical infrastructure [17]. This combination of digital and physical worlds leads to the emergence of improved services for decision-making, as well as smart campus green sustainability. Smart campus is a concept that contains a plethora of solutions, which have been implemented in several campus levels. Such levels are decomposed to smart microgrid, smart classrooms, smart laboratories, building information management (BIM) systems for smart buildings, as well as assessing students' attendance and performance through face and emotion recognition techniques and dedicated devices like smart cards. Every of these small innovations contribute to the development and realization of a contemporary smart campus along with its components. Such a sustainable campus is derived by the concept of a smart city infrastructure. In this chapter, a smart campus concept based on certain operational components is presented. Specifically, these components are analyzed to provide insight to the smart campus sustainable green ecosystem as a miniature of a smart city. In addition, it described the need for unobtrusive monitoring in smart campus infrastructure.

3.1 Smart Campus Components

Smart campus is a miniature of smart city since it is inspired from the smart city dimensions and design concepts. In addition, smart campus exploits efficiently the available infrastructure potentiality to provide a sustainable environment for students, academics, and support personnel. Nowadays, several universities and research

IoT-enabled Unobtrusive Surveillance Systems for Smart Campus Safety,
First Edition. Theodoros Anagnostopoulos.
© 2023 The Institute of Electrical and Electronics Engineers, Inc.
Published 2023 by John Wiley & Sons, Inc.

institutes have incorporated Internet of Things (IoT), edge computing, and artificial intelligent (AI) technologies to build digital campuses. Such campuses support several applications from certain research domains, which integrate with IoT devices and AI backend intelligence to provide well-being benefits to smart campus population. Teaching and progress assessment in smart campus extends the classroom and is supported both synchronously as well as asynchronously according to specific learning management systems (LMS), such as Moodle and MS TEAMS. LMS also support modular and personalized learning when combined with massive open online courses (MOOC) educational platform. Concretely, university management is also supported by smart campus activity. Specifically, smart campus is able to provide improved digital services to the academic community based on big data analytics. Such analyses aims to improve supported business processes, which contain smart building operation, public spaces environments, and human social interaction. In addition, developed and upgraded software provides cloud storage, 5G and 6G networking technology, as well as edge AI, data science, and deep learning analyses capabilities. IoT devices produce online and real-time dynamic data sources, which are used to input intelligent systems and make early warnings and predictions of certain integrated application domains. To understand the operation background of a living smart campus, it is proposed to separate five fundamental components, which describe its interoperability within both physical and digital worlds. Specifically, smart components are categorized as (1) smart grid, (2) community services, (3) campus management, (4) propagation services, and (5) campus prosperity [18]. These components are derived from certain perspective of smart campus activity, such as social, environmental, and economic sustainability. Concretely, social sustainability refers to the interaction of the campus with the human dimension perceived either as individual user or as a community of people. In addition, environmental sustainability is relative to sustainable ecosystem perspective, as well as green campus concept. Subsequently, economic sustainability is well adjusted to the employability quality of service (QoS) and the digital economic prosperity. Smart campus components are presented in Figure 3.1.

3.1.1 Smart Grid

Energy storage and reuse in smart campus is supported by smart grid. Such grid enables the campus to provide energy facilities, which might support smooth operations in the context of a daily schedule. IoT sensors and actuators provide the communication link to data generation and processing, which enable smart campus management to handle emerging operational inefficiencies smoothly. Smart grid is able to provide a significant insight to the energy flow pattern within the campus. Such a grid has the role of balancing energy reserves to assure an optimal usage of stored energy for the campus upcoming needs. For

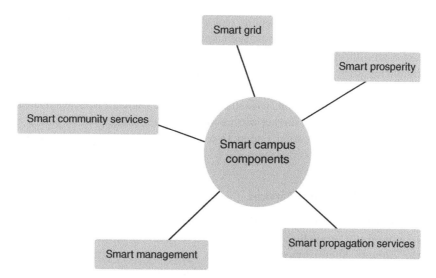

Figure 3.1 Smart campus components.

example, a smart grid can deliver services based on optimal integration of power generation processes. Usually, smart campus incorporates a low-voltage distributed system to provide services while offering certain opportunities for energy savings and storage. IoT devices embedded in the campus are able to run at different speed levels as per load. Specifically, this attribute enables smart grid to adopt to the appropriate load, as well as lower speed of the enabled processors at run time in case the workload is low or partially unused in certain places of the campus. Concretely, solar energy enables the system to adapt to climate changes [19]. In addition, IoT-enabled devices communicate in real time with the smart grid to exchange generated data sources. Electric power generated by the use of solar cells in smart parking area is used to provide power to smart campus lights and other sensors assigned to certain parking lots. Subsequently, solar cells installed in smart parking are able to harvest energy in sunny daytime and store collected energy for further use in several areas of the campus that need energy at night. There is a need for state-of-the-art smart metering systems, which will input smart campus infrastructure with adequate energy reserves for efficient operation. Such operations could be used by smart campus management service to provide statistics and predictions of future energy needs in the campus. Statistical analyses and prediction accuracy can draw energy saving and distribution policies in the smart campus. In addition, predictions might be optimized by incorporating edge AI and deep learning forecasting models to enable early warnings on future demands. There is a need to eliminate carbon emissions in the campus, which could be faced with the adoption of monitoring devices to monetize carbon emissions. Noise pollution is another problem needs to be treated in university campus. Such a problem is faced with the incorporation of a monitoring service, which alerts in case of the noise levels exceeds a threshold level. For example, noise in a laboratory can impact lecture in another adjacent classroom. Monitoring is also precious in case there is a need to detect smoke produced by individuals who smoke cigarettes. Concretely, issues related to efficient recycling and further processing of waste management compose a pillar for producing renewable energy to provide green and sustainable energy policies to smart campus ecosystem.

3.1.2 Smart Community Services

University campus' top social priority is to offer improved services to smart campus community. Certain highly importance services can be provided on real time in the campus. Such services include safe e-transactions through automated teller machines (ATM) as well as smart-card-enabled e-payment and e-wallet digital interaction methods. Industrial innovations in the area of digital economy have transcend smart cards potentiality, thus moving a step forward and support financial transactions with affective computing recognition. Specifically, affective computing is the technology, which supports facial, voice, gesture, and emotional recognition of an individual within a certain digital transaction process. Concretely, voice recognition is provided in cases of supporting live audio translation services within the classrooms and the laboratories to enable foreign students to communicate with teaching personnel. Subsequently, live data sources could input the campus dashboard to enable QoS decisions. In addition, the utility of a campus technology to count the number of students in a certain classroom provides on-time emergency recovery in case of a physical disaster, such as earthquake or fire damage. Such services are feasible due to the proliferation of sensors and actuators provided by IoT technology, which in turn feed machine learning and AI models running either in the cloud or in the fog or edge of the smart campus network [20]. Networking enables social interaction to exploit data generation potentiality within the campus to provide feedback to appropriate decision-making. However, the purest objective of a university campus is to provide high-quality education services while simultaneously supporting teaching and learning processes. Specifically, there is a need to support smart and reliable outcomes and solutions, which will lead to enhancing teaching and learning at the university campus.

Certain tools, such as appropriate LMS, could be combined during the lectures in physical world thus providing improved synchronous and asynchronous teaching services to students and campus community. In addition, authentication of a student presence in the class might be achieved by applying facial authentication with video cameras installed in the class. The opposite scenario is to assure teacher's engagement within the class to assess online the efficiency of teaching methods and materials used by the academic, which would lead to periodical reports for optimizing quality of teaching. Another area of community service is the ability of the physical infrastructure to assist students routing in real time within the university buildings through personalized beacons from embedded IoT devices. Such service could be an appropriate way of letting students know if there is any update in their daily schedule in the campus. Closed-circuit television (CCTV) system is able to enhance physical safety within the campus. It holds that such applications should be continuously updated with the state-of-the-art hardware and software technology to prevent malevolent behavior. However, privacy issues are an area which should be respected. Specifically, students should be monitored unobtrusively while private data should not be revealed, except in a case of a malicious safety's system compromise. Concretely, managerial and strategic smart campus planning is expanding beyond static processes to areas related to university transport services. Such services are able to issue certain alerts to academics, students, and supporting personnel in case of timing inefficiencies and routing changes. Subsequently, such transport information could be stored in the cloud for producing statistical reports and feeding intelligent model to early warning and prediction of a future inefficient situation proactively. Interaction of the system with the users is supported by users' smartphones and tablet mobile apps provided by the technical software development service of the university campus. Smart mobility is another service provided by smart campus by exploiting connected and autonomous vehicles (CAV) infrastructure along with advancements in campus vehicle ride sharing systems and other utilities supported by the intelligence transport system (ITS) developed in the university campus. Such ITS systems could be incorporated for resource allocation and optimal traffic flow. In addition, smart campus is a sustainable area, which protects user's well-being by adopting smart health QoS for cases of emergency within the green ecosystem.

3.1.3 Smart Management

Insights about the university campus activities can be provided at any time and anywhere due to campus management control panel. Access to such a panel is limited only to authorized users, which enter and exploit its functionality through a technically stable authentication process. Panel access is separated to classified levels according the degree of asset significance they refer to and protect, as well as the classification level of the users trying to enter and use the system. According to the classification levels, it is offered a variety of level of management services. Specifically, strategic plan is a serve provided by the campus management system for assessing system's decision-making processes. Such plan should collaborate with services related to the campus community to set the future directions of the university campus. Management system is able to provide decision-making services and to devise internal mechanisms to ensure campus business processes continuity. Concretely, the panel could be assessed by third parties and stakeholders to provide permission and access rights to users on processed campus data sources. In addition, available data could be granted to support campus policies, as well as standard operational processes. However, campus management component although it allows data access permissions it should also preserve user's privacy and safety from unauthorized malevolent users. Such a security policy should be granted and provided through adequate logging of system's activity. Such logging, needs to be managed and maintained for any potential audit and future invocation. Resource allocation and management can assist campus panel in scheduling improved processes, which could interest municipality and stakeholders' strategies for transparent aware activities [21]. Subsequently, the system could prepare and sent to parents the performance of the students along with their attendance in classroom lectures and laboratory assignments. However, campus management is not running as a stand-alone service but rather connects university daily activities with the government and other public sectors. IoT and AI technology can unobtrusively observe stress levels of campus users to provide predictive statistics for future analyses and further use.

Pollution sensors embedded in the smart campus infrastructure are able to monitor the air quality on university and make predictions when pollution levels reach a predefined threshold value. A plethora of campuses have health care infrastructure, which incorporate IoT devices such as sensors and actuators to provide monitoring of campus inhabitants and patients' health levels. Such health systems are able to take instant actions when an injury or a health incidence occurs. In case of pandemic, like the recent spread of covid-19, a health monitoring mobile application might track infected users, send them to quarantine areas, and reduce the disease spread. Concretely, AI techniques could be used for generating e-health reports by analyzing stochastic data sources and performing pattern matching and recognition of sick monitored population. Such reports could provide early warning and prediction services to the health campus system to avoid relevant situations in the future. In addition, radio frequency identification (RFID) technology provide tracking potentiality of every resource included in smart management system. This technology can track library books borrowing service online and remind students to return books after a certain period has passed. Such systems are actively used in many university campuses and have transform positively the way of life of smart campus' inhabitants by providing advanced wellbeing services. However, there is still a need for more detailed research to be performed by machine learning models to exploit more connected potentiality of generated data in campus. These data could assist the creation of a proactive management system, which might provide security campus personnel advanced monitoring capabilities to face malicious behavior from malevolent external users. In addition, such security data logs generated could provide predictive monitoring services to anticipate the extended future needs based on current monitored situations and make future safety recommendations to suppress upcoming malicious events. It is also possible to use unobtrusive surveillance capabilities to handle a variety of large campus events taking place in stadium or theaters to control campus gates' activities based on the crowd flow in the university infrastructure. Another area of campus management is the case of ITS and traffic flow within the university. Such traffic can be predicted by AI and machine learning models to sample time and divert traffic in rush hours to control and avoid traffic congestions.

3.1.4 Smart Propagation Services

Smart campus is considered as a miniature of a smart city, thus improvements in the local area of the university campus have impact in various levels of human habitation including a smart city or a consortium of smart cities within the same local government regulations. When referring to smart campus, there is intuitively a connection of such a place with dispersed smart buildings in the same area or even in distributed areas spanning to different geospatial locations that a campus might be expanded. Such distributed development of smart campuses needs to be treated by an integrated system able to schedule several processes that might run simultaneously in all or most of the university campus areas. Specifically, a smart campus should provide propagation services by being able to scale up, be reliable, and support replicability. In addition, provided services of data privacy and security as well as IoT-enabled safety infrastructure aim to provide academics, students, and support personnel a viable place to achieve high degree of effectiveness in their tasks. Concretely, it should be taken special care for the design, creation, and protection of inhabitants' digital credentials to exploit smart campus system's processes potentiality. A key vision of the university campus system is the proposal of a sustainable model, which could be able to easily integrate with local municipality government with appropriate adjustments. To achieve such a goal, there is a need for adequate security protocols, intrusion detection systems (IDS), and encryption applications to support the digital part of the smart campus. Scaling up and replication of the system should be performed with limited amount of deployment costs. Subsequently, replication of the university campus to other smart campus or smart city infrastructure should respect the privacy of the existing users during interaction with the new environment [22]. In addition, smart campus' development and deployment costs should be reasonable and simple to understand and calculated. Concretely, the cost of hardware and software technology will be increased when the replication process is achieved at a wider scale. However, an insight of potential cost that may arise could be of high significance when arranging finances for the construction of contemporary innovation projects at a smart city level. Subsequently, data produced in the smart campus independently or from various data sources should be tested for reliability before archiving and filtered in cloud storage. When a smart campus software development has reached a certain threshold, additional hardware is proposed to support high confidence of the provided data sources to the overall university campus system infrastructure.

3.1.5 Smart Prosperity

University campus prosperity is well aligned with the knowledge generation within the campus to facilitate prospective future professionals and academics toward high-quality entrepreneurships and employability. Concretely, except of provided knowledge offered in a smart campus in a variety of disciplines, another key performance indicator for the university or research institute reputation is the employability of the graduate and postgraduate students along with publications, patents, research innovations, and entrepreneurship alumni outcomes. Such research and innovation results and ideas should be commercialized to provide a business model, which fits current campus activity and future directions [23]. Such directions could be the design of an enabling digital economy model generated from the university campus and scaled up to a wider area like the local government or a vast smart city. However, it should be noted that smart campus business area is considered as a new marketplace where many investors are not always willing to invest increased capitals due to the uncertainty of return on investment (ROI) degree they will benefit from such investments in the near future. To overcome this inconvenient point on business development currently there is an opening toward proposed business models, which can attract serious investments for innovative smart campus projects. Specifically, what is recommended is to start with small projects, which is highly possible to result in immediate ROI. Focusing on this concept the investment on a paid smart parking is possible to be given high deployment priority. Such initiatives have high degree of success and can provide immediate ROI to the investors and governments, while simultaneously open the vision for further long-term projects.

3.2 Unobtrusive Surveillance Campus System

Smart campus is a living area where inhabitants are making progress in academic research and business innovations. Such environment is supported by certain components, which enable continuous development in certain areas of the university campus. Although smart campus is considered as a miniature of a smart city, this does not discourage investors to invest capital to university campus and expect significant ROI. Actually, smart campus is a protected environment, compared to a technology hub, where new ideas are produced, developed, and deployed, while scientists and stakeholders assess the potentiality of such ideas to further deploy them in a larger scale of local government, a smart city, or even to a connected consortium of university campuses and smart cities worldwide. However, analyzing all the smart city components potentiality, such as smart grid management, community services exploitation, smart management design and operation, propagation services applications, and overall campus prosperity, there is a need to preserve sensitive private data of the inhabitants. Specifically, to provide a viable and secure university campus to academics, students, and support personnel, it should be taken into deep consideration the adoption of an unobtrusive surveillance system. Such system could provide safety of university campus population in cases of malicious behavior by malevolent users. Concretely, having an unobtrusive monitoring system could lead to excellent operation and interoperability of adopted smart campus components.

4

Unobtrusive Surveillance Systems

4.1 Geospatial Internet of Things

Smart campus monitoring is enhanced by the proliferation of sensors and actuators incorporated to support geospatial Internet of Things (IoT) awareness. Specifically, geospatial location prediction, as well as time of arrival estimation, is feasible due to stochastic processes based on IoT networks [24]. In such systems, it is possible to apply a published subscribe utility to assign sensors' activity to certain geospatial data sources of observed measurements used for unobtrusive surveillance purposes [25]. Edge computing approaches focus on data collection that collects only the meaningful data from IoT devices. Such localized data sources are used to support services based on geospatial constraints [26]. Disaster management services are supported by IoT data streams, which are geospatially annotated to assist big data analytics aiming to provide campus recovery [27]. Geospatial modeling is applied to support safe students' transportation within smart campus by exploiting geolocated sensors' infrastructure design to provide a secure IoT-enabled architecture [28].

A survey on geospatial IoT is examined, in [29], which exploits context-aware personalized location-based services to provide potential geospatial analytical methods and monitor applications incorporated by smart campus physical infrastructure. An event-driven architecture is proposed in [30] that enables asynchronous transactions through campus sensor network by exploiting spatiotemporal data sources for online analytical streaming processing. Geospatial analysis is feasible to visualize and monitor campus area based on data generated by wireless IoT sensors and actuators. Such a system is used to design and maintain a safe smart campus public area architecture [31]. Location awareness is supported by a system proposed in [32], which leverages geospatial IoT-driven applications for

IoT-enabled Unobtrusive Surveillance Systems for Smart Campus Safety,
First Edition. Theodoros Anagnostopoulos.
© 2023 The Institute of Electrical and Electronics Engineers, Inc.
Published 2023 by John Wiley & Sons, Inc.

providing an integrated solution for campus monitoring. A software architecture is proposed in [33] that enables geospatial data sources analytical processing for providing smart campus integrated microservices exploited by students. Such geospatial IoT services are essential to enable efficient campus unobtrusive surveillance utilities.

4.2 Smart Campus Unobtrusive Surveillance

IoT technology facilitates the incorporation of sensors and actuators for efficient smart campus unobtrusive surveillance. In such an environment, students are monitored unobtrusively to retain privacy and human rights. Ethical and legal requirements dictate the need for students to be aware that they are being monitored to provide well-being in their working place. Monitoring of public spaces is a major deterrent against delinquent behavior, enabling a safer space for all [34, 35]. Furthermore, the motivation behind unobtrusive surveillance systems in IoT-enabled smart campus is to capture such behavior and to better understand the individual reasons and root causes. Inferences from the collected data, can then inform prevention, prediction, and early warning of delinquent behavior before this happens, acting as a security shield to contemporary smart campus life.

In this book, we survey a high number of systems in the smart campus unobtrusive surveillance domain to reveal their strengths and weaknesses. The aim is to set up the basis of classifying contemporary systems proposed in research efforts and patents according their utility in unobtrusive surveillance. However, before we are ready to provide an outcome of this survey, it is essential to compare systems based on certain research dimensions of the proposed taxonomy. To realize a comparative assessment, we proceed with the definition of a concrete taxonomy that exploits the available systems. This taxonomy will become the basis for mapping any smart campus unobtrusive surveillance system to allow comparisons with any other system found in the respective literature. Through the proposed taxonomy and the provided classification, readers and researchers will be able to identify any shortcomings in contemporary research and propose efficient methods to deal with new frameworks in the domain.

4.3 Proposed Taxonomy

The current survey focuses on research approaches that incorporate unobtrusive surveillance systems in IoT-enabled smart campus. The adoption of unobtrusive surveillance systems is depicted in our taxonomy. We report on the proposed taxonomy before we survey the existing research efforts to give the necessary overview of the domain. Hence, it will be easy to determine the main characteristics of each system and their place in the related literature.

We define the smart campus context that aims to set up the rationale for classifying unobtrusive surveillance systems. The smart campus context incorporates hardware, tools, data, software, and research methods that an unobtrusive surveillance system adopts to become the basis for realizing a solution for a smart campus. In general, IoT-enabled smart campus unobtrusive surveillance system context can be categorized into five main dimensions: (1) physical infrastructure, (2) enabling technologies, (3) software analytics, (4) system security, and (5) research methodology. These dimensions are discrete, which means that the relevant context of each system belongs only to one of the aforementioned dimensions. Our taxonomy is structured in a dimensionally specific way (i.e. we give equal attention to each dimension) to cover a range of diverse components and features. Each contextual component and feature are assigned specific values denoting their role in the proposed taxonomy. Components are related to the tools and hardware adopted in each category, while features are related to the contextual information (e.g. data) adopted in each dimension and system.

First, the physical infrastructure involves the following components: (1) sustainable smart campus, (2) smart transport, and (3) autonomous vehicles. Sustainable campus can be further categorized according to the type of infrastructure into (1) smart buildings, (2) smart classes, (3) smart labs, (4) public spaces, (5) smart parking, and (6) smart lighting. Smart transport can be divided into (1) smart traffic lights and (2) electric vehicles. Autonomous vehicles can be characterized to (1) unmanned aerial vehicles (UAV) and (2) connected and autonomous vehicles (CAV). Figure 4.1 visualizes the conceptual map of the physical infrastructure dimension.

The second dimension entails the enabling technologies of the IoT-enabled smart campus unobtrusive surveillance ecosystem, consisting of the following components: (1) core IoT technology, (2) passive monitoring technology, and (3) active monitoring devices. Core IoT technology can be further decomposed according to the type of computation: (1) IoT platform, (2) Raspberry Pi, (3) Arduino Uno, (4) wireless sensor network (WSN), (5) sensors, and (6) actuators. Respectively, passive monitoring technology can be categorized into (1) radio frequency identifier (RFID) equipment, (2) global positioning system (GPS) device, (3) Ethernet protocol, (4) Wi-Fi, (5) Bluetooth, (6) ZigBee, (7) near-field communication (NFC), (8) 4G, (9) 5G, and (10) low-power wide area networks (LPWAN), which contain technologies such as SigFox, LoRa, LTE-M, or NB-IoT [36–43]. Active monitoring devices are divided into (1) cameras, (2) microphones, (3) smartphones, (4) smart watches, and (5) automated teller

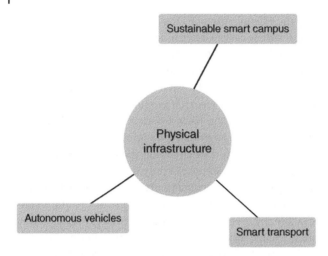

Figure 4.1 Conceptual map of physical infrastructure dimension.

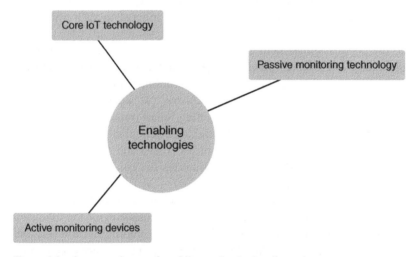

Figure 4.2 Conceptual map of enabling technologies dimension.

machines (ATM). A conceptual map of the enabling technologies dimension is visualized in Figure 4.2.

The third dimension of the proposed taxonomy, software analytics, incorporates an unobtrusive surveillance system design component that is further categorized according to its location coverage into (1) ad hoc, i.e. static, (2) mobile, i.e. dynamic, and (3) mesh, i.e. mixed location coverage. In addition, the features of this dimension spread out to (1) computing methodology, (2) affective computing, (3) user context, (4) software architecture, (5) inference system, (6) inference algorithms, (7) extended reality (XR), and (8) application. Computing methodology focuses on the computing paradigm of (1) edge computing and (2) cloud computing. Affective computing is decomposed according to the recognition of human affections into (1) voice recognition, (2) face recognition, and (3) gesture recognition. User context is divided into (1) social, (2) movement, (3) crowdsourcing, (4) crowd sensing, and (5) ambient intelligence (AmI). Furthermore, corresponding to the provided service, software architecture is characterized by (1) big data and (2) service-oriented. The inference system feature is divided according to conceptual focus and is build up by (1) context aware and (2) decision support. Inference algorithms based on machine learning and artificial intelligence approaches are categorized into (1) supervised, (2) unsupervised, and (3) semi supervised. XR according to type is separated into (1) virtual reality (VR), and (2) augmented reality (AR). Finally, the application feature branch off according to execution location type as follows: (1) desktop, i.e. static location, and (2) mobile, i.e. dynamic location. Figure 4.3 visualizes the conceptual map of software analytics dimension.

System security involves cybersecurity system component as well as specific features. Such features are (1) regulations, (2) attacks, and (3) security mechanisms. The cybersecurity system component is further decomposed into the following domains according to the safety level: (1) authentication system and (2) intrusion detection system. With regards to legal requirements, the system security

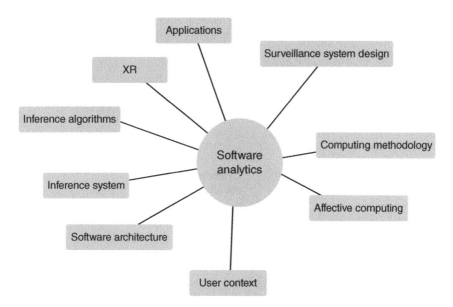

Figure 4.3 Conceptual map of software analytics dimension.

regulation feature builds up to (1) security standards and (2) privacy compliance. Attacks are divided according to their type into (1) cryptanalysis, (2) denial of service (DoS), (3) eavesdropping, (4) hacking, (5) spoofing, (6) sniffing, (7) man in the middle attack (MTM), (8) jamming, (9) data leakage, (10) password capture, and (11) virus infection. Security mechanisms can be further grouped into (1) anonymization, (2) steganography, (3) data encryption, (4) biometrics, (5) network monitoring, (6) firewall, (7) password, and (8) antivirus system [44–51]. A conceptual map of the system security dimension is visualized in Figure 4.4.

The last dimension of IoT-enabled smart campus unobtrusive surveillance system context, i.e. research methodology, focuses on the following two features: (1) research context and (2) data context. Research context regarding the time required to conduct research and the type of the research is further categorized into: (1) acquisition time, (2) quantitative, (3) qualitative, and (4) mixed. Data context according to type is decomposed into (1) real, (2) synthetic, (3) streaming, (4) batch, (5) text, (6) sound, (7) image, and (8) video. A conceptual map of the research methodology dimension is visualized in Figure 4.5.

Figure 4.6 visualizes the proposed taxonomy in a concise conceptual tree map. Specifically, the map is constructed by using the relative frequencies of the taxonomy components and features as encountered during processing certain research efforts. Concretely, the unobtrusive surveillance system category appears more frequently than the category of software analytics, thus it appears with larger font size. Subsequently, data context category appears less frequently than that of software analytics, thus it is represented by smaller font

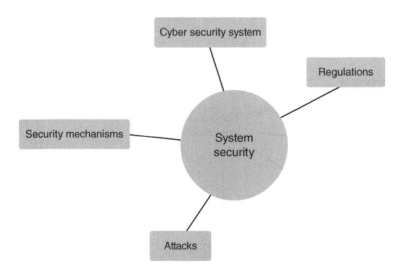

Figure 4.4 Conceptual map of system security dimension.

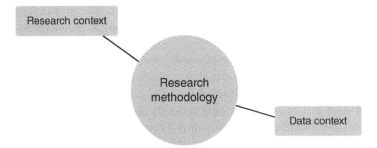

Figure 4.5 Conceptual map of research methodology dimension.

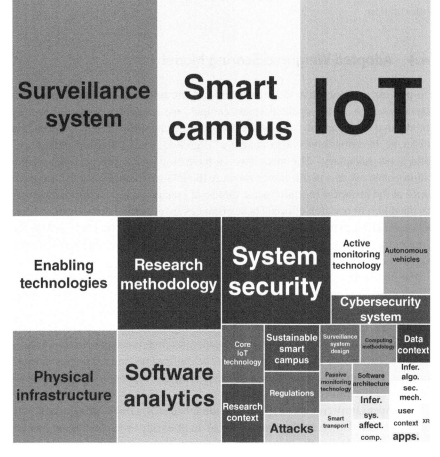

Figure 4.6 Conceptual tree map of the proposed taxonomy.

size. The final visualization is a relative frequency-based mosaic of different font size categories of certain taxonomy items and presented as a conceptual tree map.

Figure 4.7 presents an overview of the above-discussed components and features in a marked up conceptual tree graph. Specifically, components and features of the proposed taxonomy are divided into five categories (dimensions), forming a high-level description of the core concepts placed on the left side of the figure. In the intermediate levels, the emerged research component categories are presented in hierarchical order, according to the taxonomy's significance. The conceptual tree graph is completed by assigning certain features to certain categories as presented in the right side of the figure. Note that certain features are assigned to certain component categories, which means that the taxonomy is sound, and thus does not contain cross-reference misleading information.

4.4 Adopted Weighted Scoring Model

To provide a quantitative characterization of the reviewed unobtrusive surveillance research in IoT-enabled smart campus, we adopted a weighted scoring model that evaluates the value of the research and classifies them in a descending order, i.e. by using three classes, namely "High Adequacy," "Medium Adequacy," and "Low Adequacy." The taxonomy we have proposed in the previous section allows us to use as a performance measure the relative frequencies of the appearance of the instances (nominal scale values) of systems' components and features in the different research efforts. These instances are evaluated through an additive value function that incorporates a normalized weight value that is based on the importance order provided by the experts for each value of the nominal scale and its corresponding appearance frequency.

For the estimation of an overall evaluation of each research effort, a weighted scoring model is applied. As the proposed taxonomy indicates, the evaluation criteria are categorized in a structural way using a two-level categorization, namely dimensions and categories. The multilevel scoring model takes into consideration this tree structure of the criteria and incorporates preference information from a group of experts for assigning weights at the dimensions and categories of these criteria. The categories according to the taxonomy correspond to components and features of the efforts under discussion.

A compensatory criteria weight elicitation model, e.g. a trade-off approach [52], could be used. However, this would lead to an intensely time-consuming process given the number of the criteria and their categories and sub-categories, so a non-compensatory approach will be adopted.

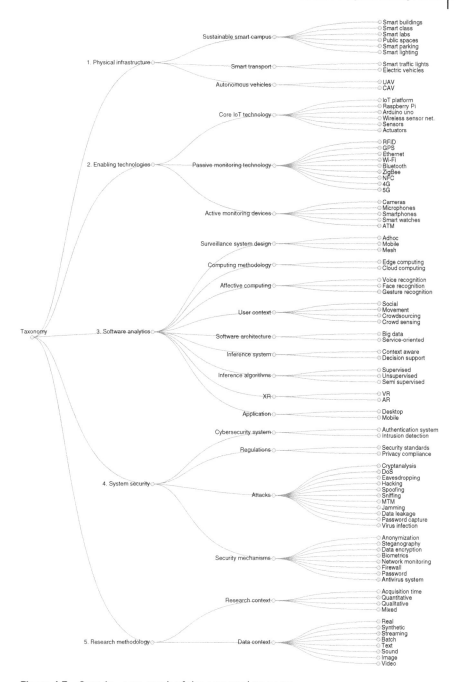

Figure 4.7 Overview tree graph of the proposed taxonomy.

Existing non-compensatory methods that are widely used to assess the criteria for the importance of weights are classified into two categories: (1) direct assessment procedures, where the decision maker or a field expert is asked to explicitly express the criteria weights in terms of percentages or determine how important a criterion is, e.g. on an absolute scale from 1 (no important at all) to 10 (very important), or on an ordinal scale, and (2) indirect methods, inferring the weights from pairwise comparisons of the criteria or reference alternatives [53]. In the second category, the methods include among others: (1) the method of cards proposed in [54, 55], (2) the method of centralized weights [56] that requests from the decision maker a number of ordinal comparisons of criteria that are formulated as linear inequalities, in order to obtain the centroid of the vertices of a polyhedron, and (3) WAP method [57] based on cards method but it includes enriched preferential information toward more robust weight vectors.

In our case and after taking into consideration the size of our classification problem and available effort from the experts, we have decided to adopt a direct assessment procedure for the assignment of weights at all levels of the structured evaluation criteria. We assign normalized weights, i.e. sum up to 1, on the dimensions and the categories (i.e. components and features).

A category can be either a component or a feature category containing either components or features, respectively. A mixture of components and features is allowed in the same dimension.

At the first level, namely the dimensions, the experts are asked to explicitly express the weights in terms of percentages. These weights shall be normalized by making their sum equal to 1. Dimensions are conceptually regarded as equally weighted, since each dimension emerges a unique niche per unobtrusive surveillance system of the proposed taxonomy. Let us define w_d, as the normalized dimension weight, then for the 5 adopted dimensions it holds that

$$\sum_{d=1}^{5} w_d = 1 \tag{4.1}$$

For the next level, namely categories, the determination of the corresponding weights is implemented by asking the experts to rank the categories for the least important to the most important. No ties are allowed. Let r be the ranking of category ca in a dimension d. After ranking the categories based on their significance within each dimension, the analyst calculates the relative importance of each category as follows:

$$w_{ca}(r) = \frac{|R_d| + 1 - r}{\sum_{i=1}^{|R_d|} i} \tag{4.2}$$

where $w_{ca}(r)$, is the normalized category weight at rank r and $|R_d|$ is the cardinality of the specific ranking R_d of a dimension d.

For the evaluation of the research efforts, we need to calculate the value of each instance in the defined categories. In each category, a specific ordinal scale is used. In order to estimate a value that will incorporate the appearance frequencies as well, we built an additive value function, assuming that it has a linear form. We asked the experts to rank the values of each ordinal scale from the best to the worst, and we assigned numeric values $v_{ca}(r)$ to each position r (1st = 1, 2nd = 2, etc.) of a ranking R per category ca as follows:

$$v_{ca}\left(r\right) = \frac{|R_{ca}| + 1 - r}{|R_{ca}|} \tag{4.3}$$

where $|R_{ca}|$ is the cardinality of the specific ranking R_{ca} of a category ca. $v_{ca}(r)$ is the normalized value (e.g. max value is 1) of each ranking position r.

In order to incorporate the appearance frequencies of each value of a category, we need to calculate the relative frequencies of its appearance in the research efforts. The meaning of relative frequencies is to count and then normalize the frequency of a specific value to occur in a certain category. Let us define f_v, as the normalized relative frequency value, then for the total number of the g_{ca} values of a certain category, it holds that

$$\sum_{v=1}^{g_{ca}} f_v = 1 \tag{4.4}$$

So, the value of a specific research effort i concerning specific nominal values $v_{ca}(r)$ in a category ca is calculated as follows:

$$v_{ca}\left(i\right) = \sum_{r=1}^{|R_{ca}|} v_{ca}\left(r,i\right) \cdot f_v\left(r,i\right) \tag{4.5}$$

where $f_v(r, i)$ is the relative frequency assignment for the ranking position r of the instance of i and $v_{ca}(r, i)$ is the normalized value for the ranking position r of the instance of i in a certain category.

When all the taxonomy data has assigned with certain relative frequency values, we feed them to the weighted scoring model to receive the overall evaluation of each research effort i. Let us define $v(i)$ as the overall value of each research effort i. Then for the overall evaluation of each research effort, it holds that

$$v\left(i\right) = \sum_{d=1}^{5} w_d \sum_{ca=1}^{e_d} w_{ca} \cdot v_{ca}\left(i\right) \tag{4.6}$$

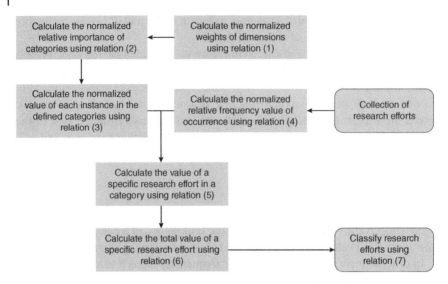

Figure 4.8 Work flow diagram of the proposed scoring model.

The necessary classification will be performed through the comparison of the overall values of the research efforts to some value thresholds that define the lower bound of each class, as follows:

$$\begin{cases} v(i) \geq v_H \Rightarrow i \in C_H \\ v_H > v(i) \geq v_M \Rightarrow i \in C_M \\ v_M > v(i) \Rightarrow i \in C_L \end{cases} \tag{4.7}$$

where $v_H > v_M$ are thresholds defined by the experts in the global value scale [0, 1], after the calculation of the values of all research efforts, to discriminate the groups. v_H is lower bound of group C_H (research efforts with High Adequacy) and v_M is the lower bound of group C_M (research efforts with Medium Adequacy). The selection of the thresholds is related to the specific values that have been calculated for the 44 research efforts in order to assign 10 efforts under the category "High Adequacy," and 10 more under the category "Low Adequacy." The remaining research efforts will lay in the category "Medium Adequacy."

Research efforts i, with a value v_i greater than v_H, are regarded as the best efforts and are the proposed solutions of the survey.

Figure 4.8 shows the flow diagram of the classification algorithm that is proposed by the authors in this section that is based on direct assessment procedures for expressing the importance of the various levels of the taxonomy elements.

5

Smart Campus Safety Systems Survey

The research efforts are surveyed, corresponding to the proposed taxonomy in this study, are compared, and their strengths and weaknesses are clearly stated. These research efforts cover more than 10 years of research in the area of Internet of Things (IoT)-enabled smart campus surveillance systems. There were surveyed 42 papers and 2 patents, covering all the dimensions of the proposed taxonomy. The distribution of research outputs by year of publication is presented in Figure 5.1. Specifically, from 2008 to 2012, the annual research yield is rather sparse. Instead in years 2016–2021, it is observed a more systematic research approach in the published literature, indicating the maturity of the research community toward surveillance systems for smart campus, from an IoT perspective. Based on the survey results, it is performed a classification of the reviewed systems.

5.1 Systems Not Classified

Researchers in [58] propose a system that develops a smart campus where every place in the campus is connected to a central Wi-Fi control unit. This was achieved by incorporating IoT technology to provide automation, security, and surveillance services to students and the university personnel. The system focuses on smart buildings and smart lighting surveillance, while it incorporates electric vehicles infrastructure. It also uses IoT platform, Arduino Uno, wireless sensor network (WSN), sensors and actuators core-enabling technologies. To provide passive monitoring services, it incorporates radio frequency identification (RFID), global positioning system (GPS), Ethernet, Wi-Fi, Bluetooth, and ZigBee technology. In addition, active monitoring is achieved with cameras and smartphones. Quality of

IoT-enabled Unobtrusive Surveillance Systems for Smart Campus Safety,
First Edition. Theodoros Anagnostopoulos.
© 2023 The Institute of Electrical and Electronics Engineers, Inc.
Published 2023 by John Wiley & Sons, Inc.

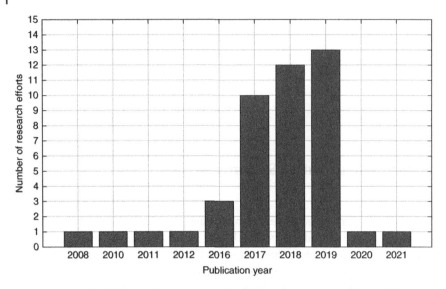

Figure 5.1 Surveyed research efforts per year of publication.

service (QoS) is assured with an ad hoc surveillance system, enabling context awareness through supervised inference algorithms. An intrusion detection system is incorporated, which complies with security standards. The system handles man-in-the-middle (MTM) and password capture attacks through extensive network monitoring, firewall setup, and password security mechanisms. Authors worked with mixed research methodology, while data used are real life and streaming. Data types used for the experiments were text and video.

Specifically, a system architecture is proposed, which is based on a concrete multilayer architecture adopting a very low-cost Arduino Uno micro-controller, IoT sensors and actuators, as well as RFID technology. An open-source platform is incorporated for hardware design, analysis, and testing. In addition, assisting software implementation is used to support and exploit micro-controller's computational potentiality. Data produced by the sensors and IoT devices of the adopted architecture are further fused to feed software models to provide safety services. Subsequently, each physical place of the smart campus is equipped with appropriate hardware devices, which are exploited by certain software programming scripts running at the edge of the supported network. Safety and privacy services are assured with the incorporation of password protection through a user-friendly graphical user interface (GUI) to assist university campus users. Concretely, system's components are synchronized in certain time periods to enhance safety procedures. In addition, system's knowledge base is secured in the cloud and updated in a daily basis, while updates are informing, unobtrusively, terminal users through their smartphone mobile applications. Subsequently, proposed system architecture preserves real-time surveillance services, which are feasible without loss of important data. Furthermore, the system's service provider is responsible for the QoS of the proposed architecture as well as the supported maintenance procedures, which are performed periodically.

Experiments of this approach are performed in the area of smart buildings, smart lighting, and electric vehicles surveillance within smart campus with real equipment of Arduino sensors and RFID technology. Results are promising and tend to be incorporated my more areas within smart campus. However, there do exist scalability issues in testing the approach to the wide area of the campus due to upcoming complexity to required components. Overall, it is an interesting use case where real equipment is used to test the robustness of smart buildings surveillance consistency; however, new areas should be examined to extend the current test bed.

In [59], a system that enables smart campus safety based on RFID technology is presented. The system uses Tabu search to find the optimal places in the campus to deploy the RFID readers to provide students' surveillance services. The research mainly focuses on smart class and public places surveillance, while core technology includes an IoT platform, WSN, and sensors infrastructure. Passive monitoring is achieved with RFID and GPS sensors, while students' smartphones are used for active monitoring. A mobile surveillance system is designed, based on cloud computing, while inference is based on supervised algorithms running on mobile smartphone applications. The research incorporates an intrusion detection system compliant with security standards. The system handles denial of service (DoS) and hacking attacks with the incorporation of biometric security mechanisms. A quantitative research method is used and it is stated the acquisition time of the research to completion. Text data is produced and streamed from the smartphones.

Specifically, it is proposed an agent system, which supports RFID applications for smart campus safety. Adopted system architecture is divided in two separate layers, where the first layer contains the superior in higher hierarchy RFID reader, while the second layer is composed by a reading speed adjustment mechanism for anti-collision. First layer uses Tabu search to estimate backscatter power, while the second layer use this information to find optimal locations for deploying the incorporated readers. Concretely, Tabu search process uses dynamically the power control approach to calibrate power coverage of reader, while further avoiding reader-to-reader collisions. It is assumed that RFID readers are deployed within a certain target area in the smart campus. The adopted RFID-based framework is designed to provide safety and privacy services to the university campus' actors, such as academics, students, and personnel. Given the proposed system orchestration, there are provided certain unobtrusive surveillance services such as (1) campus gate management service, (2) student temperature anomaly management service, (3) hazardous area management service, (4) campus visitor management service, and (5) campus equipment management service. Adopted RFID technology further supports a smart campus architecture to guarantee users safety by incorporating supportive IoT technology. Such a system is composed by certain operational frameworks, which are (1) physical network interoperable framework and (2) assistive software framework. Subsequently, both frameworks are cooperating to provide smart campus privacy and safety QoS.

Real-life experiments are performed within the campus by incorporating RFID technology to exploit smart class and public spaces surveillance systems. Proposed system is able to sense students entering dangerous areas in smart campus as well as to distinguish campus visitors apart from student population. Large numbers of RFID tags make system hard to manage efficiently, which is obviously a limitation. Overall, the system is well designed and proved to be able to protect users' personal safety within the campus; however, a more detailed design should be done to provide a less-complex RFID tag infrastructure.

Authors in [60] introduce a system that uses Arduino Uno and wireless technology to provide necessary smart campus security and surveillance. The proposed system is focusing mainly on public spaces and smart lighting areas of the university campus. It incorporates an IoT platform to process available Arduino Uno, WSN, and sensors' data produced in the campus. Smartphone GPS sensor is used as passive monitoring technology and cameras are used to capture images of the surveillance area. The surveillance system is established on a mesh infrastructure based on both ad hoc and mobile nodes that enables gesture recognition of the suspicious subjects. User movement context inputs supervised inference algorithms to enable surveillance services running on mobile smartphone applications. The system incorporates both an authentication and an intrusion detection system complied with certain security standards. Such security systems can treat hacking attacks by using password security mechanisms. A quantitative methodology is used to evaluate real streaming image data produced by smartphone cameras.

Specifically, proposed research effort supports certain surveillance systems deployment principles, such as (1) hard-wired surveillance system, (2) wireless surveillance system, and (3) remote access surveillance system. Concretely, hard-wired surveillance system incorporates wires, which are used to connect sensors and closed-circuit television (CCTV) cameras. Wireless surveillance systems use battery-powered radio transmitters and receivers to connect cameras and sensors. Remote access unobtrusive surveillance systems can be accessed from distant locations far away from the surveillance area. Such systems provide reliability, portability, high performance, and end-to-end safety services. Proposed system is composed by a combination of the supported surveillance systems technical potentiality. An Arduino Uno and dedicated sensor technology, which provides more reliability than other existing systems is adopted for deployment. In addition, adopted system provides certain multipurpose surveillance services, which can be applied in various physical areas within the university campus where edge network security is required. Proposed system is composed by certain hardware and software components. Concretely, hardware components of the adopted system are (1) Arduino Uno, (2) passive RFID sensors, (3) GPS module, (4) CCTV cameras, and (5) assistive computers. Subsequently, software components of the proposed system are (1) Microsoft Visual Studio, (2) C programming language, (3) C++ programming language, (4) Python programming language, and (5) Node.js, and VB.NET.

The system is tested with real data in laboratory setup exploiting Arduino sensors technology. Results emerged the need of a light infrastructure for applied smart campus surveillance systems. Experiments, however, mainly focused on image capturing and video analysis. Extending potentiality of the system is its ability to detect users' behavior activity and perform face recognition. Overall, it is a solid approach; however, at the current stage it needs further experiments to exploit its potentiality.

Researchers in [61] propose a system that analyzes human behavioral data to provide surveillance services to students during their daily life on the smart campus. Analyzed data is also evaluated by system administrators to provide certain positive social impact to the university. The system is mainly applied for smart buildings as well as smart labs and public spaces surveillance areas. Core IoT enabling technologies used by the system include sensor devices, as well as GPS and Wi-Fi passive monitoring techniques. Active surveillance monitoring is achieved with the proliferation of cameras and smartphones as part of an ad hoc integrated system. The system incorporates social, movement, and crowdsourcing user context to provide surveillance services. Supervised inference algorithms run in mobile applications to output a decision support system for QoS surveillance. Authentication mechanisms and intrusion detection systems enhance the effectiveness of the proposed research, consistent with current security and privacy regulations. The system can handle sniffing attacks by using network monitoring, firewall, and antivirus system countermeasures. Acquisition time of the mixed research methodology is provided, and data used are mainly batch and synthetic videos.

Specifically, the smart campus unobtrusive surveillance system focuses on online processing of campus data sources to infer users' behavior and stochastic life style. Analysis is focused on individual users' as well as on groups of users' behaviors. In case of individual users, the study aims to provide recommendations in the area of humanistic care services. Instead, in case of groups of users' behavior analysis is based on dense activity data sources provided by the adopted system. Subsequently, based on the experimental data sources, the system is able to provide accurate data visualization methods to perform descriptive statistics graphs and charts for inferring individual students' behavior. Such knowledge is then used for providing end users certain advices regarding their observed campus activities. In addition, utilizing unobtrusively the university campus, and the students' social networks interactions produce accurate data sources, which is feasible to analyze the relevance between different data sets and provide recommendation system utilities for covering emerging students' social needs. Concretely, daily life activities, which are produced by certain e-cards, Wi-Fi locations, e-mail context, and social network interactions, are stored in log data sources. Such data sources are further used for analytical processing to provide specific methods to understand human behavior in several areas of the university campus. Subsequently, a concrete methodology is adopted to engage with machine learning methods to construct a user's life-style reporting system for student's unobtrusive surveillance. In addition, other analytical methods are incorporated to build a recommendation system able to serve daily users' needs in the campus. Concretely, the adopted safety system uses a ground truth research method, which aims to conduct a study in more depth over human behavior while simultaneously preserving student's privacy and safety by providing an incentive mechanism to engage with willing full smart campus students.

This approach uses synthetic data to perform certain experiments. Results are promising in defining the context of surveillance life-style report system based on students' data from the campus. However, the fact that the data used for analyses are synthetic is a limitation of the current system in case it is considered to be deployed on a real-life experimental setup. It is a well-formed approach with safe and sound research methodology; however, in its current form it lacks the real ground truth setup that would be used for further evaluation.

In [62], a system is introduced that uses IoT technology and devices to provide a sustainable smart campus surveillance environment. Specifically, the system focuses on smart labs and public spaces, as well as with smart parking and smart lighting surveillance areas. Core enabling technology covers IoT platform, Raspberry Pi, Arduino Uno, sensors, and actuators devices. Passive monitoring is feasible due to the incorporation of RFID sensors as well as Bluetooth, ZigBee, and near-field communication (NFC) network communication protocols. Cameras and microphones are used as active monitoring devices for efficient campus surveillance. The proposed surveillance system has an ad hoc design and incorporates cloud technology to achieve face and gesture recognition. User movement context was sent to unsupervised inference algorithms, enhancing the functionalities of mobile surveillance applications. Research exploits the potentiality of incorporating an intrusion detection system, which covers certain security standards. The system can handle sniffing and password capture attacks with a variety of data encryption and firewall security mechanisms. Acquisition time of the adopted quantitative research is defined, while data used are real and streaming. Sound, image, and video data are all incorporated.

Specifically, the proposed smart campus system methodology incorporates the deployment of multiple sensors including soil moisture sensors, ultrasonic sensors, and cameras, which are connected and controlled through Raspberry Pi hardware module. In addition, other sensors are also used like infrared sensors and microphones, which are connected to Arduino Uno processor. Sensors sense certain physical quantities and transform them to digital signal, which is then transmitted to the cloud of the adopted system for further processing. Such system supports certain functions like smart canteen and smart library, which are accessible by the smartphone mobile applications used by the campus students. Each time a request happens, it is processed by the system while simultaneously the knowledge base is updated to provide efficient services. In addition, proposed unobtrusive surveillance system supports certain services such as (1) smart street lighting, (2) smart parking, (3) smart automation, (4) smart gardening, (5) smart air quality, (6) smart noise monitoring, (7) smart weather monitoring, and (8) smart office, provided services. Facing multiple emerging needs of the system raise issues, which should be treated instantly to assure robustness. Such issues are decomposed to (1) object naming for dealing with different services, (2) data conversion to treat connected components compatibility, (3) interoperability of devices, (4) QoS based on the transferred application data streaming between the system and the users, (5) facing security attacks to protect users and devices form malevolent behavior, (6) data encryption and key management to ensure data protection, (7) security of hardware to mitigate risk of physical infrastructure compromise, and (8) treat network congestion to handle data transmission loss on real-time requests.

Although the study proposed a compact initial system, for experimentation in the final stage, the researchers used a subset containing mainly the Arduino processor and the connected sensors. The results in this limited edition of the proposed system were positive; however, the limitation of not having more components deteriorates the integration of such system in real scenarios. Overall, the rationale behind the experimental setup is interesting, but the experiments should be repeated with a superset of the current experimental setup.

While the past studies provided some interesting findings, further research in surveillance systems is required. Specifically, in [58], new areas should be examined, extending the current test bed into smart traffic control and integrated smart surveillance systems architecture. Since large numbers of RFID tags make the system hard to manage efficiently, a more detailed design should be done to provide a less complex tag infrastructure [59]. The solution developed in [60] could be extended to include current surveillance system that detect students' behavior activity and face recognition captured from multiple data sources within the smart campus. Experimentation, in [61], with real data sets would lead to more robust results that could be further used by prospective researchers. Future research in [62] should be focused on resolve interoperability of integrated devices with heterogeneous functionalities toward a smart environment.

5.2 Systems That Focus on Public Spaces and Smart Parking

In [63, 64], researchers adopt surveillance systems that focus on public spaces and smart parking. Specifically, in [63] the authors propose a computational cognitive modeling approach to understand and design a mobile crowdsourcing system for improving campus safety and reporting. The system uses an IoT platform to process data produced by the incorporated sensors located in the smart campus. Sensor communication is achieved by Wi-Fi passive monitoring technology and the system also exploits data captured by cameras and user smartphones. The designed surveillance system is mainly mobile, exploiting cloud-computing utilities to process social, movement, and crowdsourcing user context. A big data architecture is used to input data to a decision support system (DSS) for inferring an incident based on a supervised algorithm that runs on mobile devices. The system incorporates both authentication mechanisms and intrusion detection techniques for system security, which are standards compliant. Spoofing attacks are faced with the adoption of specific password security mechanisms. Acquisition time of the quantitative research methodology is defined, while the data used are real and batch. Data types processed by the system include text and video.

Specifically, proposed system provides crowdsourced reports to assure users' safety and privacy. Crime reporting and the associated under-reporting issue is discussed and supported by the adopted unobtrusive smart campus surveillance system. Such reporting is decomposed to victim reporting, which has impact in victim's behavior. Concretely, these behaviors are prone to the (1) seriousness of the crime, (2) recorded demographics, (3) university campus public areas' victimization, and (4) perceived costs and mutual benefits of reporting a malevolent behavior. In addition, the system exploits the potentiality of witness reporting, which is mainly based on the (1) offender's characteristics, (2) witness characteristics, (3) victim as well as offense characteristics, and (4) situational variables affecting the reporting process. Subsequently, university campus reporting is treated as a wholistic process, which is supported by the adopted system. Such reporting is based on unobtrusive monitoring to reduce on-campus severe crimes. Reporting process is considered to include not only violent crimes but also other types of crime incidents, like theft and stultify against a campus student. Inclusion countermeasures should be applied by the university policy makers to treat such kind of offensive crimes, which might be more prevalent among campus students. Adopted research effort also performs a comparative study on the theoretical foundation of crime reports, while certain surveillance systems, which are able to face safety and privacy threats, are analyzed. Concretely, there is a significant contribution on the psychological motivators, which enable user engagement to face malicious behavior in the university campus.

Laboratory experiments were performed exploiting mechanical Turk (MTurk) environment. Results enhanced the understanding of different human factors that may have an effect in students' commitment to share safety reports. The study applied on a smart campus with certain student population. Experiments were based on hypothetical scenarios where the responses were self-reported and thus may be biased. Overall current research is well designed and evaluated; however, incorporating experiments could optimize it based on real-life scenarios.

In [64], the authors present a system that introduces a security responder framework to reinforce smart campus safety and reduce surveillance costs. The system also adopts unmanned aerial vehicle (UAV) infrastructure. An IoT platform, Raspberry Pi, WSN, and sensors are used as core technology to enable the proposed surveillance system. The system uses 4G for data communication, and RFID and GPS sensor are also incorporated. Active monitoring is supported with the exploitation of cameras, microphones, and smartphones, forming a mesh surveillance system design. Cloud computing is used to process social and user movement context to provide context awareness. Inference algorithms are used to include supervised and unsupervised techniques and the system incorporates mobile applications. Authentication and intrusion detection systems, which comply with privacy regulations, are used to face virus infection attacks. Network monitoring is the basis of the security mechanism to face malicious threats from the surrounding environment. Acquisition time of the quantitative research methodology is defined, and data used are real and streaming. The data types processed by the system include text, sound, images, and videos.

Specifically, adopted system incorporates IoT technology to define a framework able to provide safety and security services in a smart campus. Proposed framework supports certain operations to manage university campus applications. Such applications are conceptually grouped in several areas of interest like (1) intelligent building interoperability to provide a green ecosystem; (2) smart campus grid to handle electric power, water supply, and energy sharing sustainable resources; and (3) learning environment enhanced with e-learning features to provide an articulated place for learners based on students' aspirations, knowledge exploration, and talent skills. Subsequently, a safety and security system also proposed as a fundamental part of the adopted framework, which is based on a multilayer architecture incorporating sensors and actuators embedded in the university campus. Adopted system is able to detect certain types of attacks, such as (1) illegal gun position, (2) assault malevolent behavior, (3) burglary activities, and (4) firing arms malicious incidents. Safety and privacy of the system is assured with the adoption of certain IoT devices, such as cameras, microphones, glass break sensors, Raspberry Pi, UAV technology, and a dedicated server connected to the smart campus control center. Concretely, the adopted safety system is trained and tested over a certain period of time with various malicious incidents, which enable it to predict stochastically a malevolent behavior in the campus. Such delinquent behavior is then suppressed accordingly by predefined security processes control by the campus center.

The research is based on laboratory experiments. Results indicate that finalizing the implementation of the proposed system may improve its capability to achieve an optimum performance. However, applying a vast number of sensors in the smart campus is possible to make the configuration of the technical parts a challenging issue. In addition, limited financial resources of universities will be a trade-off in applying such a complex system. The architecture is well defined; however, it does not explain how it will face possible forceful opposition from students on the smart campus regarding the invasion of their privacy.

Although significant work has been done, there is a need for further research in the area of surveillance systems that focus on public spaces and smart parking. Future research, in [63], will focus on a more diverse set of participants expanding the narrow area of the smart campus to experimentation in the wide area of a smart city. Refined information provided by the proposed system, in [64], would lead to an early prediction of crimes and future prevention.

5.3 Systems That Focus on Smart Buildings, Smart Labs, Public Spaces, and Smart Lighting

Authors in [65, 66] introduce smart campus surveillance systems that, focus on smart buildings, smart labs, public spaces, and smart lighting. Specifically, in [65], researchers propose a smart system based on a smart card biometrics approach that can be integrated to a university campus providing contemporary surveillance services. It incorporates an electric vehicle physical infrastructure. The system uses a wide range of enabling technologies including IoT platform, Raspberry Pi, Arduino Uno board, WSN, sensors, and actuators located in several places in the campus. Passive monitoring is achieved with the incorporating RFID sensors as well as Ethernet, Wi-Fi, ZigBee, and NFC communication protocols. The surveillance system is ad hoc based mainly on cameras technology. Cloud-computing processes exploit social context to provide surveillance QoS, and it incorporates desktop and mobile applications. Security is based on authentication mechanisms and intrusion detection systems, which comply with privacy regulations. Sniffing attacks are handled with the adoption of network monitoring security mechanism. The research method used in this effort is quantitative and data used are real and streaming text.

Specifically, proposed monitoring system adopts a variety of services to assure efficient surveillance of the university campus. A smart card service is used by the system, which is based on a mini-computer able to store and process multimodal data sources. Such service is mainly incorporated by the university for a variety of system activities. Proposed system also supports a smart waste management service, which collects waste from the campus and then recycle inorganic materials as well as further process organic waste to compost dumps in the smart city. Subsequently, smart bins of the university campus are equipped with weight, volume, temperature, moisture, and smell sensors to trigger an alarm when the bins are full of waste. In such a case, dedicated waste trucks collect only the full of waste bins, thus reducing carbon dioxide emissions. Dynamic scheduling and routing directions given to the waste trucks have significant impact to the smart campus green and sustainable quality of life. Concretely, smart microgrid services adopted by the proposed system are responsible for decentralizing electric power to further achieve reliability and decentralization of energy resources in the campus. Subsequently, smart lighting service aims to reduce university campus high consumption of energy by applying IoT technology sensors and actuators within the campus public spaces. In addition, environment analysis service is provided, which measures air quality through pollution sensors embedded in indoor areas of the campus, such as smart classes, laboratories, and corridors. Such service is based on a reporting process, which is able to log quality of air environmental sensor values to provide a green smart campus environment. Concretely, security and safety services are incorporated in the proposed surveillance system architecture, which treat malevolent users' behavior in the campus area. Subsequently, an automation service is responsible to provide support in students' daily life in the university through automated devices within the campus.

At the current development phase, experiments have been performed in a limited area of the implemented services. Results have been observed for the fields of environmental analysis, smart lighting, automation, and proposed security system. Lack of implemented services to perform further experiments is a limitation of the effort. Overall, it is a promising research work, which evaluates the proposed system; however, more experiments should be done to effectively assess the observed results.

In [66], researchers introduce a conceptual surveillance modeling of smart campus as a system, composed by certain smartness levels of the campus sustainable components. The system is based on IoT platform, WSN, sensors, and actuators, and it incorporates RFID and Wi-Fi passive monitoring technology. Active monitoring is achieved through cameras, microphones, and smartphones that form an ad hoc surveillance system. Cloud-computing processing is used to provide voice and face recognition. Big data architecture is incorporated to feed the supervised algorithms with data to infer an incidents. The system also has VR and AR capabilities while it is built on mobile applications. Both an authentication mechanism and an intrusion detection system are used to protect the smart campus, according to certain security standards. In addition, anonymization, biometrics, and network monitoring security mechanisms are used. Conducted quantitative research methodology has defined acquisition time of completion. Data used are real and batch, and data types are sound, image, and video.

Specifically, the adopted system defines a conceptual model of the smart campus, which is able to identify and classify fundamental features, components, relational links between the supported components, interfaces, input and output data streams, as well as certain limitations and constraints during interaction with the university environment. Concretely, proposed system incorporates efficient software applications, hardware devices, pedagogy principles, teaching and learning activities, as well as emerging safety services, which are vital for the campus unobtrusive monitoring operation. In addition, adopted system classifies certain structural conceptual abilities according to a variety of smartness' levels. Such inherent conceptual abilities are summarized to (1) adaptation as an ability to modify physical or behavioral features to interact with the university environment; (2) sensing and awareness, which is the ability to identify, recognize, understand, and become aware of a certain context; (3) inference and logical reasoning as the ability to infer logical conclusions based on multimodal data sources, which are processed accordingly based on explicit or implicit evidence, rules, and observations; (4) self-learning as the ability to acquire new knowledge or similarly modify existing experience, which aim to improve behavior performance, skills, and efficiency; (5) anticipation is the ability of thinking or reasoning exploiting top-down and/or bottom-up reasoning principles, which enables prediction of what behavior is more possible to be observed in certain time slot in the future; and (6) self-organization and re-structuring optimization as the ability of an unobtrusive surveillance smart campus system to alter its inner structure with regards to building components, as well as regenerate and self-sustain under certain prosperous conditions without interact with external entities.

Experimental setup of this effort is toward conducting conceptual modeling and system description of surveillance systems. Results prove the need of surveillance in the concept of Smart Campus though analytical experiments based on student population. The limitation of this effort, at the current phase, is the lack of integration of such system in real environment. It is a solid research based on real data sources; however, more work should be done toward the adoption of such system in actual campus' surveillance system.

Systems of this category can undertake more future research work. Specifically, in [65], authors can extend their effort toward an integration of electric vehicle charging stations and smart structural health systems exploiting data generated from campus sensor nodes. Multiple components to support the proposed system, in [66], is required, aiming to maintain distinctive surveillance features as well as dealing with software applications heterogeneity.

5.4 Systems That Focus on Public Spaces and Smart Traffic Lights

In [67–69], researchers adopt surveillance systems that focus on public spaces and smart traffic lights physical infrastructure. Specifically, in [67], the authors present a system that analyzes the implementation of certain security mechanisms to provide a sustainable smart campus ecosystem. Such system is composed of an IoT platform, which processes data produced by WSN and sensors located in the campus public spaces. Passive monitoring technology incorporates RFID and GPS sensors, while active monitoring is achieved through installed cameras, and all together form an ad hoc surveillance system. Big data architecture is running on the cloud, it is defined a DSS, and it is based on supervised and unsupervised inference algorithms running on desktop applications. Authentication mechanisms and intrusion detection systems provide security and privacy to users. The system faces DoS, data leakage, and password capture attacks with the proliferation of anonymization, data encryption, and biometrics prevention mechanisms. The adopted methodology is mixed including quantitative and qualitative analysis performed on a given research acquisition time period. Real and streaming text data are used for experimentation.

Specifically, proposed system performs a constitution analysis of smart campus, which is decomposed to certain dimensions like (1) management, (2) scientific research, (3) security, (4) technical platform, (5) convenient life, (6) green campus, and (7) teaching. Management dimension is further analyzed to automatic work as well as student and personnel management. Scientific research is composed by research and papers' management. Security dimension is decomposed to security protection and vehicle management. Technical platform is responsible for data center continuous operation as well as students' and personnel digital identification. Convenient life dimension is further analyzed to smart card utilities and smart library services. Green campus is responsible for smart irrigation and smart illumination. Concretely, teaching dimension is composed by teaching and resource management, practice teaching methods, and smart classrooms' utilities. In addition, smart campus is also enabled with IoT technology, which is composed of (1) a sensing layer, (2) a transport layer, and (3) an application layer. Subsequently, sensor layer is further divided into: (1) RFID and quick response (QR) code technologies, (2) GPS support, (3) sensors and actuators devices, and (4) video unobtrusive surveillance mechanisms. In addition, transport layer is analyzed for (1) mobile communication network, (2) computer network, and (3) mesh network technology. Concretely, application layer is responsible for (1) data mining processes, (2) search engine efficiency, (3) cloud data management services, (4) robust processing platform, (5) terminal applications, and (6) user friendly web services. Another principal characteristic of the adopted system is the security constitution of the supported IoT infrastructure, which is divided into (1) sensing layer security, (2) transport layer security, and (3) application layer security. Concretely, in sensing layer, there are (1) RFID security, (2) sensor network security, and (3) data collection security. Subsequently, in transport layer supports (1) gateway security, (2) transport security, and (3) network and information security. Subsequently, application layer safety is composed of: (1) storage and management security, (2) calculation security, and (3) privacy security.

Research is performed by laboratory experiments based on real data. Results assess the quality of sensors along with the use of fiber-optic sensors to replace electronic sensors. The system also enhances privacy protection technology for wireless sensor networks. In addition, more work should be conducted for providing a viable solution for the transport and application layers security problem. Overall, real data is used to evaluate the system; however, more experiments should be performed to provide a robust outcome of the research effort.

The authors of [68] present a system that illustrates an ontology for IoT-enabled smart campus architecture. The system also introduces a continuous data processing unit, which is used for online reporting. Proposed system incorporates WSN, sensors, and GPS as key enabling technologies. Surveillance system is ad hoc and it is based on cameras located in public spaces of the campus. The system focuses mainly on decision support process, incorporating virtual reality (VR) supervised algorithms, running on desktop applications. Security standards are followed, and authentication mechanisms as well as an intrusion detection system are both incorporated to provide certain levels of security to users. Virus infection attacks are prevented with the adoption of an antivirus system. The research methodology is based on quantitative approach. Data used for experimentation are real and synthetic text data.

Specifically, adopted system proposes a framework, which will not only monitor smart campus students but also focus on identifying interests of a learner thus providing an intelligent platform to analyze students' activities. Such platform is also convenient for assessing certain university campus individuals' behavior. The system incorporates IoT technology to assign certain physical objects' identities to convenient digital entities. Such digital entities are able to be processed and further provide decision-making services, which have impact to the systems' digital world. Concretely, proposed system adopts a wireless mesh network to support physical network potentiality by incorporating high-coverage network facilities, which is provided by the university campus. An ontological approach is used to specify the design of the IoT-based system. Such an approach includes certain diagrams, statement, and logical expressions, which enable system performance as well as easy specification and reengineering of the adopted models. It is fundamental that the university campus supports coverage with an advanced sensor network technology. Such network technology enables IoT devices to be connected to the wireless mesh network as well as to the wired network infrastructure of the proposed system. Subsequently, wearable sensing devices are mobile and continuously active, while dedicated sensors are tuned to monitor and track in real-time students' movement and various activity. Concretely, such information is further used to update online the dynamic knowledge of the supported university campus system. Subsequently, proposed unobtrusive smart campus surveillance system is able to get instantly information from the safe and sound logical supported ontology to further process students' movement and social activity within the university campus.

Experiments are based on certain future plan exploiting various interests and skills. Results evaluate the proposed ontology presented with graphical diagram and mathematical analyses. Proposed research work has limited functionality and theoretical approach, which is not yet implemented. In addition, it has a plenty of dimensionality in design part for deeper presentation, as well as implementation level. Overall, it is a solid effort, but more implementation required presenting its potentiality, especially in the area of adoption and analyses of psychological and learning user attributes.

In [69], researchers introduce a system, which is based on participatory sensing using smartphones to collect and process local student data to monitor the smart campus. The system is also able to infer students' activities during daily schedule by identifying user trends and stochastic behavioral patterns captured by sensors located in the campus. Specifically, GPS sensors as well as 4G and 5G technologies are used for passive monitoring. Smartphones and smart watches are incorporated to perform active campus monitoring. The proposed system is mobile and uses cloud-computing capabilities to evaluate social and movement user context. A big data architecture is used to feed data into supervised and unsupervised inference algorithms running on mobile applications. An intrusion detection system protects the system by monitoring all its activity as a second-line defense, while password capture attacks are confronted with the incorporation of data encryption and network monitoring security mechanisms. Acquisition time period of the research is defined, and the research methodology followed is quantitative. Furthermore, real and streaming text data are used for the experimentation of the system.

Specifically, a participatory sensing unobtrusive monitoring smart campus system is proposed in this research effort, which collects data from sensors embedded within the university. Such system's sensors are located in several mobile equipment like in the smartphones, smart watches, and various other wearable devices. Subsequently, smart surveillance system merges data sources produced by these devices to infer students' trends and behavior performed at certain time within daily activity. Activities monitored are walking, running, biking, and vehicle driving. Students and personnel's activities are further combined with inherent contextual information encoded in the system, such as temporal context and GPS locations within the university campus. Concretely, unobtrusive surveillance smart campus intelligent system is able to analyze the flow of users, which are currently located in the university campus. In addition, adopted system can identify behavioral trends, as well as certain stochastic patterns based on many situational factors of primary interest. Produced information could be incorporated to improve and modify QoS levels offered to the individuals, such as privacy and safety assurance services. Subsequently, proposed monitoring system also motivates positively users to persuade them to change their behavior by engaging them to use green and sustainable modes of transport, such as bikes, skates, or public transport instead of using private vehicles. Concretely, adopted system achieves such positive user behavior changes by providing them incentives to exploit contemporary gamification techniques potentiality.

The proposed effort performs experiments based on real data of the system that exploit the research area of participatory sensing to improve services provided on the campus. Current results focus on the extraction of system features from fixed length time windows, which feed a classifier to perform user activity recognition. More features should be incorporated to the classification schema to observe higher values of system effectiveness. Overall, the proposed system is efficient exploiting current implementation in terms of accuracy, precision, and recall metrics.

Future work is vital to expand the findings observed during these research works. Specifically, in [67], more work should contain research that focuses on strengthening network security as well as protecting personal privacy in the sensing layer. Research, in [68], should incorporate experiments with power and saving mode, which could be considered for defining adopted devices sustainability. In the future, in [69], a mechanism for sharing local data by users should be tuned, especially in cases where there are users who intentionally send corrupted data to deteriorate QoS. In such cases, reputation management techniques should be adopted.

5.5 Systems That Focus on Smart Buildings and Smart Classes

Authors in [70–72] introduce smart campus surveillance systems that focus on smart buildings and smart classes. Specifically, in [70], researchers propose a system that uses the Open Authorization (OAuth) protocol to allow secure authorization from third-party applications to access online surveillance services.

The proposed system uses an IoT platform and sensors technology, as well as RFID and GPS to provide online services. It also incorporates cameras to achieve active monitoring of the university campus. In addition, the surveillance system is based on a mesh architecture using cloud-computing capabilities to evaluate social context. The system incorporates both desktop and mobile applications. Regarding the security dimension, an intrusion detection system, which complies with security regulations, is established. The system can handle password capture and virus infection attacks with the adoption of a password authentication mechanism and an antivirus system. Mixed research methodology is used combining quantitative and qualitative methods. Data used are real and streaming, and the data types incorporated in the study are text and video.

Specifically, adopted system incorporates OAuth, which is am open license agreement protocol able to provide a safe and reliable working framework for engaging third-party user applications to access HTTP service according to certain authority and privacy limitations. Using OAuth for connected devices has the advantage of providing significant support to certain libraries, API platforms, and client developers. Proposed surveillance system incorporates OAuth to provide the university campus a robust authentication system architecture. Such architecture is composed by three separate layers, namely (1) infrastructure layer, (2) application service layer, and (3) information provision layer. Concretely, infrastructure layer is responsible to collect and further processing provided data sources according to certain time limitations. Processing in this layer should be as accurate as possible exploiting RFID technology, infrared sensors, and GPS potentiality. In addition, infrastructure layer is collecting information by dynamic monitoring processes and then sending this piece of information from the hardware devices to the predefined data security component of the system architecture. Subsequently, application service layer efficiently integrates and manages various information to achieve unified management of processed information. Such layer is based on the existing management systems, like (1) staff management system, (2) logistics management system, (3) scientific research management system, (4) student management system, (5) financial management system, and (6) equipment management system. These systems incorporate cloud-computing capabilities and cloud storage technologies to provide a unified management platform, which is able to facilitate third-party applications development. Concretely, information provision layer is responsible for providing academics and students a specific and efficient service platform, which focuses on sharing teaching and research resources' context to form an interconnected shared software entity. Such entity aims to be accessible by all smart campus users from every place and any time during daily activity engagement within the university campus.

Proposed research conducts security experiments and theoretical analyses on laboratory real data. The system is running stably and credibly, as well as it is flexible and easy to integrate with the existing smart campus service. In addition, unified management of user information should be treated with regards to certain ad hoc experimental policy. Overall, the current research effort provides a secure and reliable framework for third-party applications considering certain strengths and limitations.

In [71], authors present a system that incorporates RFID technology to build a smart campus. A prototype of this system is introduced that takes into consideration maintenance services of electrical equipment as well as smart security locks of the university classes. The proposed system integrates smart traffic lights infrastructure. It uses RFID sensors and cameras, which communicate through Wi-Fi, Bluetooth, and ZigBee wireless protocols, to provide surveillance QoS. The adopted system is ad hoc and analyzes user movement context in the area of the campus while it is running on desktop applications. An authentication security system is incorporated, which confronts with security regulations. Cryptanalysis attacks are prevented by the system with the adoption of data encryption security mechanisms. The research method used for the completion of the effort is quantitative. The data used are real and streaming text sources.

Specifically, proposed system incorporates RFID technology to identify university campus individuals or assigned objects. Unobtrusive monitoring smart campus system is able to track and log certain patterns of interest relative to (1) employee attendance record management, (2) employees equipment tracking, (3) room safety, and (4) automation of electrical appliances. System architecture incorporates various actors and object assets, which should be tagged appropriately. Concretely, each employee should be tagged having unique identification number, such as roll numbers provided by the monitoring system process. Subsequently, various office objects will be tagged incorporating RFID labels. In addition, offices, smart classrooms, and smart laboratories should be assigned a unique identification number, which will be stored in an RFID reader device. Moreover, RFID reader devices should be placed at strategic areas within the campus, like (1) RFID reader device will be placed next to the door of each room, (2) reader device will be also placed at the university entrance and exit locations, (3) campus cafeteria and common places will be equipped with reader devices, and (4) smart laboratories and smart classrooms will also have a reader device at the entrance and exit points. Concretely, efficiency of the proposed system is assessed by conducting experiments with certain use cases within the university area, such as (1) experiment with employee and student identification, which is the primary task of the adopted system, (2) experiment with tracking of person and equipment, where both employees and students can be tracked based on their last known location, (3) experiment with room automation, which is used to handle power conservation and also track malevolent behavior, (4) experiment with smart attendance maintenance through check-in and check-out time duration of users' physical presence in the campus, and (5) experiment with avoiding theft of costly equipment where a report is performed to the system, which is able to search and find the missing object based on its last known location in the smart campus.

Current research effort encompasses a well-designed laboratory experimental setup, which is based on real data from RFID tags. Results prove that object tracking time and consumption on energy is decreased when credibility of attendance record and security of rooms are increased. A limitation of the current work is that most of features provided by the system could not be quantified after longer operational use. Overall, in the adopted effort, certain experiments estimate the average electrical power consumed in a room with high efficiency; however, more experiments required to scale up the system coverage area.

Researchers, in [72], propose a system that uses an encryption approach to provide advanced protection of students' privacy. It handles time-range encryption to maintain a user traces utility. Specifically, the core IoT technology incorporated in this system covers sensors and actuators infrastructure. Passive monitoring is achieved by Wi-Fi wireless communication while active monitoring is based on smartphones adoption. The proposed system uses mesh surveillance architecture and the computation is performed locally at the edge components. Students' movement context is evaluated and inserted into supervised algorithms that run on mobile smartphone applications. Authentication mechanisms and intrusion detection systems are incorporated to provide advanced surveillance services. The system complies with security and privacy regulations. Data leakage attacks are addressed with the use of anonymization, data encryption, network monitoring, and password security mechanisms. A quantitative research method is used to complete this effort. The data incorporated are from real and streaming text sources.

Specifically, adopted unobtrusive surveillance system university campus safety incorporates an encryption-oriented approach, which is applied in a secure framework where data are encrypted once being captured. Data source processing is performed according to a privacy preserving mode. During this process, encrypted data are not revealed in plaintext to the data processing server. Incorporated design is able to provide a much stronger protection of user privacy compared with anonymization techniques. However, the difficulty, which should be surpassed, is that encryption process applied to wireless network traces are prone to time-range volatile specification during the encryption, like the time range that a device is associated with a Wi-Fi access point. In addition, incremental nature of the time should be treated accordingly to assure the utility and correctness of the traces. Proposed system faces this inefficiency by formulating a safe time-range matching problem, which is then solved optimally. Such optimization is based on a stable quantization technique, which is also enhanced by a delegatable pseudo random function (DPRF). Concretely, the problem could be described as dealing with a trace, which contains private identity as well as spatial and temporal information that needs to be protected from malicious treats. Adopted system uses such an encryption technique to preserve user privacy, which provides provable safety while being simple and practical to use. System architecture is designed to allow legacy client applications to be incorporated directly by providing a transparent data encryption process to the client. Proposed architecture contains certain structural components, such as (1) a client, (2) an application server, (3) a proxy, and (4) a data server. Concretely, client initializes a plaintext query from a certain application, which is then passed to the application server. Data server handles the encrypted data by storing them to a dedicated knowledge base. Subsequently, stored data are further processed by a proxy, which is equipped with encryption keys. Such proxy processes ciphertext data as an intermediate between a client application and the data server. In addition, a certain adaptor is used by the data server as the appropriate middleware to support certain operations, which are provided by standard knowledge base queries' processing.

The performed experiments consider an encryption-based approach, providing stronger protection of user privacy. Results indicate that the adopted approach leads rather to moderate increase in network bandwidth, storage, and computation overhead. Scalability issues should be also examined to assess the overall efficiency of the proposed system. Overall, the adopted effort provides a research direction that incorporates encryption instead of anonymization for preserving user privacy in wireless environments.

Future work should be done toward the integration of the proposed research approaches. Specifically, in [70], it should be examined with more realistic use cases how the proposed system has a universal reference and significance with regards to the authentication and authorization process applied on the smart campus. More work is required in [71] where it is planned to expand the effectiveness of the system with biometrics and additional control equipment for campus surveillance purpose. Future work in [72] will focus mainly on expanding the proposed prototype to support other applications as well as investigating the possible use of multiple proxies in the system infrastructure.

5.6 Systems That Focus on Smart Buildings, Public Spaces, Smart Lighting, and Smart Traffic Lights

Researchers in [73–75] propose surveillance systems that focus on smart buildings, public spaces, smart lighting, as well as smart traffic lights infrastructure. Specifically, in [73], the authors present a smart public safety system that is composed of contemporary surveillance equipment, a back-office system with a workflow engine, and a mobile application for students. All the components are synchronized with an IoT platform, while passive monitoring is feasible due to GPS and 4G technologies. In addition, the system incorporates surveillance cameras and students' smartphones. Surveillance system combines both ad hoc and mobile architectures while it can perform face recognition based on movement user context. The system runs in mobile applications. An intrusion detection system is used that complies with security and privacy regulations, and a network monitoring security mechanism is incorporated to handle malicious attacks. A quantitative research methodology is used, while experiments are based on real and batch video data.

Specifically, proposed system adopts a mobile application, which connects the community of academics, personnel, and students in the university campus. A CCTV unobtrusive surveillance system collects data from various individuals' activity in the campus and inform smart campus control center to further process potential problems, which might arise in the university. In case of an emergency situation, immediate recovery actions are performed while the system is responsible to reduce false alarms, estimate optimal response time, and define certain costs associated with a specific selected action. Incorporating mobile applications in users' smartphones bring certain benefits in the interaction with the campus control center, such as (1) knowledge about user current location provided by GPS, (2) current timestamp of a system report, (3) transmission of visual information by using CCTV cameras, (4) transmission of audio and text context, and (5) direct contact with safety mechanisms through smartphone connection. In addition, mobile application can be used by every individual of the campus having a personal university identifier. Such identifier provide specific solution to improve individuals' safety as well as connecting them to a better environment by incorporating a collaborative action process. Concretely, using the mobile application individuals could expect immediate response from the university campus control center while they can also repost problematic situations online. Such online problem reporting process contains annotations to physical damages in the campus public spaces like water leakage and illumination malfunctions. When a report has been submitted to the control center, it is scheduled a maintenance process to fix the problem on real time. Subsequently, smartphone's mobile application main objectives are to (1) improve communication between the individual and the university control center response time; (2) provide safety to the academics, personnel, and students; (3) assist university's safety staff to eliminate response time in case of an emergency; and (4) create a collaborative users' community inside the university campus to assure users security and protection of the smart campus physical property.

Experiments performed on the campus where smart cameras are deployed to provide surveillance services with a mobile application interface. Results suggest that the system is able to optimize university community safety. Maintenance of the proposed system is a challenging issue and needs to be examined in follow-up experiments. Overall, the system is well deployed and tested; however, more research should be done to achieve better maintenance services.

The authors of [74] introduce a sustainable smart campus system that integrates IoT technology and big data architecture to provide surveillance services. The system also uses distributed and multilevel data analysis to find a reliable and efficient solution for implementing a sustainable university campus environment. An IoT platform along with sensors and actuators are incorporated. Passive monitoring is feasible due to RFID sensor technology, while active monitoring devices include surveillance cameras located in the campus. Surveillance system design is ad hoc and enhanced with edge-computing technology that enables voice and face recognition based on social movement and crowd sensing user context. Big data architecture inserts data into a DSS that incorporates supervised algorithms to enhance surveillance QoS. The system uses both desktop and mobile applications. The adopted surveillance system features an intrusion detection system that complies with security and privacy standards. Eavesdropping attacks are tackled by anonymization, biometrics, and network monitoring countermeasures, adopted by the proposed system. Acquisition time for mixed research methodology completion is defined within this effort, while the data used for experiments are real and batch, and the incorporated data types are text, sound, image, and video sources.

Specifically, adopted unobtrusive surveillance campus system proposes a transition from traditional campus to smart campus. Such campus incorporates the following structural components: (1) the acquisition of the big data based on IoT technology, (2) the centralization of these data in an appropriate infrastructure, and (3) the efficient management of the information, which is generated within university campus. Concretely, sensor devices are responsible for unobtrusive monitoring of all events, which are observed in the environment. In addition, sensors on a certain incident should send appropriate information to smart campus knowledge base storage system. Such system stores all the information collected in a secure and private cloud where all data are processed accordingly and transformed to appropriate distributed data sources. Big data supported architecture is responsible to select certain piece of information, through data analysis processes to provide smart campus the necessary knowledge to make secure decisions. Proposed system is able to manage the different IoT devices with regards to previous analyzed data sources from the smart university campus to provide a green and sustainable environment. Subsequently, results observed by the adopted system allow the generation of a user-friendly environment where university individuals have their needs covered by certain smart campus QoS potentiality. Dedicated system analyses could make possible to determine with high accuracy the appropriate places, which are more frequently used by campus individuals, thus specific data sources could be captured by wireless network system's infrastructure. Exact knowledge of individuals' locations makes possible to take advantage of smart campus places to generate context awareness campaigns focusing on the use of available resources. Concretely, technological advances are able to modify near future and create new paradigms on campus individuals' interactivity with underlying technology, which leads to the integration between technological advancements and their applications in social environments. Such significant areas of human interaction promotes the generation of intelligent environments, which are able to support autonomous processes, remote control, and decision making in smart university campuses.

Experiments of tuning certain parameters through simulation were performed based on real data exploiting campus operation. Results set the standards for real environment implementation that represent the system as a socioeconomic organization. Such system approach aims to consider university campus as small-scale testing environment. A limitation of the current study is the absence of system integration to scale up in the whole smart campus. Overall, it is a promising research effort that helps to define certain system standards for further implementation on campus, however scaling to the whole campus environment is required.

In [75], the authors propose a name data networking (NDN) IoT university campus system, leveraging on connected devices and students' contents to provide efficient surveillance services. Specifically, an IoT platform, WSN, sensors and actuators core-enabling technology are all used to support the proposed system. Passive monitoring is achieved with the incorporation of RFID sensors, Ethernet, Wi-Fi, Bluetooth, and ZigBee wireless communication protocols. In addition, surveillance cameras and smart watches are used as active monitoring devices. Surveillance system design is mixed, combining ad hoc and mobile techniques, running on the cloud according to a certain big data architecture. The proposed system focuses on context-aware inference of incidents and incorporates supervised and unsupervised algorithms. The system uses only mobile applications. The authentication system assures authorized access control to the system and cryptanalysis attacks are prevented by using data encryption and network monitoring security mechanisms. The research method used is qualitative, and acquisition time period is defined. Experiments are based on real and streaming data, and the supported data types supported are from text, image, and video sources.

Specifically, proposed system incorporates IoT technology in every operational area of the university campus. Smart campus is physically characterized as a single building or a combination of buildings, which utilize numerous smart sensors like (1) temperature sensor, (2) humidity sensor, (3) pressure sensor, and (4) proximity sensor. Concretely, a smart campus except of sensors also incorporates certain actuators, such as (1) lights, (2) fans, (3) doors, (4) windows, (5) vehicles, (6) smartphones, and (7) alarm buzzers. In addition, connectivity through IoT devices is enabled by network technology like (1) Ethernet, (2) Wi-Fi, and (3) Bluetooth to provide anytime and anyplace campus connectivity. Subsequently, campus server (CAS) is responsible to provide devices' connectivity as well as monitoring of all campus activities, such as controlling software agents. NDN is based on IoT smart campus (IoTSC) application, which could provide several services, like (1) energy management, (2) safety, and (3) privacy to the university infrastructure. Concretely, the adopted system proposes the exploitation of an NDN-based hybrid naming scheme (NDN-HNS) to name certain contents and IoT devices considering optimal features from information-centric networking (ICN) naming schemes to provide a green and sustainable university campus environment. In addition, ICN naming schemes are holistic, where each name is assigned to a specific content according to three discrete components, such as (1) IoT application prefix, (2) hierarchical, and (3) flat-hash and attribute based. Adopted naming scheme may provide safety, scalability, addressing and naming services to data contents, and IoT devices. Subsequently, IoTSC can assure certain university campus services, such as (1) optimization control of green energy usage, (2) safety of faculty and students' vehicles, (3) security and privacy of smart campus individuals, (4) easy access to available physical and digital resources, (5) smart cafeteria services, and (6) students' social behavior analyses. Concretely, further supported services might contain (1) early warning, prediction and management of physical disasters, (2) smart attendance system, and (3) smart timetable management system. Majority of services can be achieved by using simple operation of connectivity among smart devices, while other services might be accomplished by incorporating smart mobile applications, such as (1) software development, (2) cloud computing, (3) AI, (4) algorithms, and (5) neural networks.

Experiments focused on real-life data while further processing and testing were used to design an appropriate NDN for the studied campus. Results mark out the lack of a reasonable naming and addressing mechanism in the developed system. Experimental setup has limited resources with regards to examined network nodes and available data. Overall, it is an interested research work that proposes an NDN based on Hybrid Naming Scheme (NDN-HNS) for IoT-enabled smart campus.

Current research is well performed; however, there is a need for future work to bear down on the observe findings. Specifically, the system proposed in [73] should scale in an integrated environment of a smart campus. More work is required in [74] to include methods for enabling student population to accept the leading technological changes as part of the proposed automation process. Future work in [75] aims to evaluate the proposed system for aggregating provided data to better assess user satisfaction rate on system's services.

5.7 Systems That Focus on Smart Buildings and Smart Labs

In [76–79], surveillance systems that focus on smart buildings and smart labs are proposed. Specifically, in [76], the authors present a cyber-range platform that evaluates various real-world cyber threat scenarios to provide an unbiased security assessment of information and automation control systems for smart campus surveillance. Core-enabling technologies that are incorporated include an IoT platform, WSN, and sensors located in the university campus. Communication protocols used as part of the passive monitoring technology are Ethernet and Wi-Fi, while students' smartphones are used for active monitoring of the campus. The surveillance system design is mobile and exploits cloud-computing capabilities. The system uses movement students' context to insert data into a context awareness inference system based on supervised and unsupervised machine learning algorithms and running on mobile devices. A network-based intrusion detection system is incorporated. Acquisition time period of research completion is defined, and the effort deploys a qualitative research methodology. The data used are real and batch images.

Specifically, proposed unobtrusive surveillance system is based on cyber range technology. Concretely, it is presented an online correlation of host level event in cyber range service (C2RS) method. Subsequently, C2RS implements an out-of-band data source capturing process to achieve greater malicious attack resistance. Such resistance, utilizes a virtual machine introspection technology, which uses the methodological approach to enable C2RS to isolate data captured from distributed monitoring security hosts in the university campus environment. In addition, C2RS incorporates the captured data and input them into the volatility framework to aid in simplifying the data analyses of the operating system memory data structures. To treat training data sets of the context-aware cybersecurity situations emerged by certain cyber-range activities, a specific object-dependent method is proposed to observe the required evidence of malevolent activity. In addition, adopted C2RS method is also scalable and robust, which enables proposed system to be more applicable to specific safety tasks. Subsequently, the adopted out-of-band data-capturing module is further used into a distributed virtual network layer for providing information to data acquisition analysis layer, which will be processed by a dedicated event correlation safety engine. Concretely, the defined software object-dependent process is incorporated for analyzing the observed evidence of illegal activity, which is also used to reconstruct intrusion detection realistic use cases for further experimentation with malicious user-centric scenarios.

Experiments performed test out-of-band data focusing on attack resistance with the use of a virtual machine introspection technique. Results obtained propose an object-dependent method to analyze the evidence of illegal activity. Note that if the time range is not limited, the process of evidence vectors may refer to different threads that results in insufficient system accuracy. Overall, the study proposes a scalable and robust system; however, correlation of host-level events needs to be further examined.

In [77], the researchers propose an identification and authentication system for smart campus surveillance based on RFID and smart cards biometrics technologies. The proposed system also supports synchronous and asynchronous data-processing capabilities to provide security services to the university campus. Specifically, RFID sensors, Bluetooth, and NFC wireless communication technologies are incorporated. Active monitoring is feasible due to the adoption of surveillance cameras and students' smartphones. The design of the surveillance system is ad hoc and able to perform face recognition. A DSS is used for inference of an incident based on supervised algorithms. The system incorporates desktop applications. An authentication mechanism and an intrusion detection system are established to ensure students' uninterruptible use of a secure system that provides efficient security services. Password capture attacks are prevented with the incorporation of an antivirus system. A firewall keeps the internal network safe protecting it from external untrusted networks. The research methodology used to accomplish the effort is quantitative, and the data used for the experiments are real and streaming. The data types of the sources incorporated are text and images.

Specifically, adopted system is focusing to the university area and campus management with regards to RFID technology, which enables the incorporation of identification and authorization processes. Such systems' security processes are able to provide authorization to access a variety of important smart campus' physical and digital resources. Design of the proposed system is divided into two separate fields. The first field is assigned to provide verification of students in examination rooms. To achieve such goal, an RFID technology is used to enable a first step identification of the student population, which is present in the examination period. A second-step biometric authentication with smart cards is adopted synchronously to avoid students' blocking at the door of the examination room. Such biometric authentication process performs an anonymous verification in the systems' server side to ensure the true identity of the students. Concretely, second field is responsible to deal with the control of access to sensitive areas of the university campus. This field also uses RFID technology for identification as well as a synchronous and asynchronous biometric authentication method, which is based on pattern matching. Such matching is responsible to compare the captured fingerprint with (1) the one stored in the smart card and (2) another one stored remotely on a fingerprint server. Based on the contemporary technological advancements, the adopted system incorporates RFID technology to provide safety to certain areas within the smart campus. Such areas include (1) general campus access, (2) access to the administration office, (3) access to the library, (4) access to professors' offices, (5) access to smart classes, (6) access to smart laboratories, and (7) access to the examination rooms.

Performed experiments exploit two use cases based on how much the proposed system security could be improved by combining RFID and smart cards technologies. Observed results of the first use case focus on the performance of the verification process with student population using synchronous and asynchronous techniques. In the second use case, the focus is shifted on the security of accessing smart campus sensitive areas. In addition, system should exploit individual user context and move toward an integrated campus environment. Overall, it is a robust framework that combines RFID and biometrics technologies; however, more experiments required to scale up the adopted system.

The authors in [78] present a smart campus surveillance system that makes use of RFID and GPS technologies to promote student's well-being in an efficient learning university environment. The proposed system uses WSN as IoT-enabling technology, while surveillance is carried out by cameras located in the campus and smartphone devices supporting active monitoring. The surveillance system design is ad hoc and evaluates the user movement context to insert data into an adopted DSS. Such a DSS is built on a supervised machine learning algorithm and incorporates mobile smartphone applications. An intrusion detection system is included to ensure compliance with security regulations provided by biometrics and network monitoring security mechanisms to confront MTM attacks. Acquisition time period of research completion is provided, and the research methodology followed is quantitative. The data used for experimentation are from real and streaming text sources.

Specifically, proposed system aims to treat cases where university campus students are performing malicious behavior, such as drinking, fighting, and conducting theft incidents. Unfortunately, there exist students acting irrationally by fighting at smart campus, which actually affects rational students' learning process. On daily basis, occurrence and frequency of notorious individuals' actions affect overall students' quality of life within campus. These factors have an incremental important impact on students' phycology. University campus is not only a place of study, it is also a channel to find and train talented persons who might be the future generation's professionals and academics. Smart campus unobtrusive surveillance system provides evidence to campus safety personnel and public security officers to fight delinquent behavior within the university places. To face such a major problematic situation, it is incorporated contemporary IoT technology with certain sensors and actuators devices. Such intelligent technology implies that the application of IoT-enabled infrastructure to the smart campus backbone can enhance real-time monitoring QoS of the campus activities. Based on the stability and safety measures provided by smart card readers embedded in the university campus, adopted system exploits the potentiality of RFID and GPS technologies. Such technologies constitute fundamental components of the provided security architecture, which is used to face certain students' malevolent behavior.

Experiments are performed with real laboratory data toward an exploratory research based on RFID and GPS communication technologies. Results present that the proposed system security can prevent safety accidents effectively. Research is limited to small-scale spatial granularity. Overall, campus security based on IoT technology can be achieved; however, there is much research required to adopt such a system by student population.

In [79], the researchers propose a surveillance system that adopts edge-computing potentiality to achieve real-time student monitoring. The system explores the feasibility of Harr-Cascade feature extraction technique and support vector machine (SVM) classifier at the edge devices, while it introduces a lightweight convolutional neural network (L-CNN) to enable human detection. Specifically, an IoT platform, Raspberry Pi, WSN, and sensor technologies communicating with Wi-Fi wireless networks are incorporated. Active monitoring is based on cameras located in the smart campus. The surveillance system design is ad hoc, and computation is used at the edge devices. The system evaluates social user context handled by big data architecture. A DSS is designed to adopt supervised, unsupervised, and semi-supervised machine learning algorithms in order to infer possible suspicious incidents. The proposed system incorporates mobile applications. An intrusion detection system is established to preserve user security and privacy. Incorporating network monitoring prevents MTM attacks. This effort uses quantitative research methods based on real and streaming data sources. Adopted data types for performing experiments include images and video data.

Specifically, adopted system incorporates edge computing as a service to assure unobtrusive surveillance in smart campus. Edge-computing technology is able to migrate more computing technologies to the lower layer of the connected IoT devices, like (1) sensors and (2) actuators, at the edge of the network. Actually, edge computing is a widely used technology for campus surveillance systems since it possesses the following four advantages compared to cloud computing. First, it supports real-time response, which means that applications or services are directly executed on-site and/or near-site. In addition, communication delays are minimized, which is essential to delay sensitivity for mission control tasks, such as university campus surveillance. Second, it has lower network workload on raw data generated by sensors or monitors. Such data are consumed at the edge of the network instead of being outsourced to a remote cloud center. Furthermore, the processed results might be sent to the cloud for further analysis, where the communication overhead is much lower than outsourcing tasks to the cloud. Third, it is observed lower energy consumption, where most of the edge devices are energy constraint. Associated algorithms deployed at the edge are lightweight to reduce energy consumption for the processing and data transmission in total. Fourth, it enhances data security and privacy since less data is sent, thus fewer opportunities are available to malicious activities to compromise the confidentiality and integrity of the processed data sources. Furthermore, it is easier to apply safety and privacy policies at local network level in comparison with requested collaboration among multiple network domains under several administration units. Proposed system adopts edge-computing potentiality to provide more intelligence to campus monitoring service, which significantly improves many tasks like object detection and tracking. Incorporating the recent advances on machine learning it is adopted an L-CNN algorithm to perform human image classification and prediction with high prediction accuracy. Such algorithm has been specifically redesigned to cover the limited computational resources of edge-computing environments.

Experiments are performed in the context of edge-computing environment based on gathered real data. Results are promising with regards to the fact that the proposed system is able to track human movement with adequate accuracy in real time. More research should be performed to assess the proposed system accuracy by providing new unseen instances to optimize its accuracy. Overall, adopted research provides a decent system used to track malicious human activity; however training phase should be expanded to incorporate more real data.

Based on the observed results, it is evident that significant work should be done. Specifically, in [76], future work should include methods for improving the system's performance as well as reducing the required memory usage. In addition, a distributed computing deployment should be built. In [77], additional experimentation is needed with further technologies to ensure a highly accurate authentication, such as cameras and motion sensors. Further research work, in [78], should focus on extended experiments to deploy the proposed system in the whole smart campus environment. Further work is required in [79], establishing a proactive surveillance system that will enable campus safety by identifying suspicious human activities as well as raising early warning alerts.

5.8 Systems That Focus on Smart Buildings and Public Spaces

In [80–88], researchers propose surveillance systems that focus on smart buildings and public spaces. Specifically, in [80], the authors introduce a surveillance care and guiding framework that incorporates deep learning-enabled facial recognition. The deployed smart campus safety system is called "Deep Guiding" and uses video trajectory derived from campus students to infer malicious behavior. The system is based on an IoT platform, WSN, sensors, and actuators contemporary technologies. Active monitoring is feasible due to RFID and GPS sensors as well as Wi-Fi, Bluetooth, ZigBee, and 4G wireless data communication protocols. Surveillance cameras enable online active monitoring of the student population moving in the campus. The surveillance system design is ad hoc and exploits cloud-computing capabilities to perform face recognition with the proliferation of efficient supervised and semi-supervised algorithms, which compose a DSS, to infer abnormal behavior. The system is incorporated only into mobile devices. An intrusion detection system is also used as a second line of defense, and data encryption techniques prevent attacks. A quantitative research methodology is used to accomplish the effort, and the acquisition time period is defined. The data used by the system are from real and streaming video sources.

Specifically, proposed smart campus care system is based on a guiding framework, which incorporates deep learning models to achieve face recognition. Such system infrastructure exploits students' behavior through IoT technologies, which use outdoor localization based on GPS capabilities. Indoor positioning is also available by exploiting beacon technology potentiality along with adopted surveillance cameras. Proposed unobtrusive monitoring system is able to automatically classify observed video data streams of each students' activity to certain facial context. Such system's property can effectively achieve accurate video footprint review for a specific smart campus' student performing several activities in the university campus. Concretely, adopted system could provide time-effective indoor as well as outdoor guiding in the smart campus to accurately find a certain place to be reached, a friend to be met, or a student to be cared for further safety analysis. Subsequently, proposed system is able to alleviate temporal-consuming labor overhead to find a certain target or event of further interest in a vast amount of video streaming data sources. Such system's feature could reduce significantly overall searching time required is a smart surveillance campus to localize a certain point of interest. In addition, the overall goal of the adopted system is to achieve seamless and instant indoor as well as outdoor navigation for academics and students in the university campus by facing the next research issues, like (1) fast campus guiding, (2) accurate facial detection, (3) deep facial detection, and (4) individual video streaming classification. In case of fast campus, guiding system aims to treat up-to-date positioning in both indoor and outdoor campus areas, thus being able to plan the fastest trajectory from the current position to certain destination in an optimal manner. Subsequently, in case of face detection accuracy, system focuses on precisely detect certain students' faces observed by the online video streaming provided by monitoring cameras in the campus. Instead in case of deep face detection, special treatment is given on the correct recognition of the individuals' by using deep learning models advanced technology on optimal classification capabilities. Concretely, in case of individual video classification adopted system aims to automatically classify and store in certain software directories recognized individuals' activity in the university campus captured by video cameras.

Experiments are based on the implementation of an Android-based surveillance system tested on real data. Results show that the proposed system achieves a seamless indoor and outdoor navigation between buildings in the campus for efficient face recognition. Proposed system should be used in more areas of the campus than only in smart buildings and public spaces. Overall, it is well-designed system that keeps additional construction cost low by utilizing existing surveillance infrastructure in the campus.

The authors in [81] propose a smart campus system designed to reduce the reaction delay in reporting incidents regarding their occurrence time, by developing a mobile application. This application enables users to send alerts, directly from their smartphones to the nearest police department which include their real-time location. Specifically, the system focuses on indoor localization incidents by incorporating an IoT platform, GPS sensors as well as Wi-Fi and Bluetooth passive monitoring technologies. Such a system is based solely on students' smartphone devices to enable a mobile surveillance system design. Cloud-computing processing evaluates user movement context to provide context-aware information of the university campus. Machine learning supervised algorithms that run on mobile applications are incorporated into the solution. An intrusion detection system is included that complies with user-centric security regulations, and sniffing attacks are prevented with the adoption of an anonymization security mechanism. This effort is accomplished using a quantitative research method. Experiments are performed using real and streaming text data sources.

Specifically, adopted unobtrusive surveillance smart campus system develops a mobile application, which enable users to send alerts along with their actual position to the university campus police department directly from their smartphones. Simultaneously, adopted mobile application may be used to cover other areas in the smart campus without using standalone phone infrastructure. In addition, when a student sends an alert signal through the mobile application, the university police department is able to capture current position of the victim's smartphone along with previously stored data sources, such as (1) student's profile picture, (2) name, and (3) age. Accordingly, university police department is able to monitor the victim's real-time position in the wider smart campus area visualized on a certain web application. Subsequently, this visualization is active until the problematic situation is being solved. Upon the incident is solved, tracking of certain student will be turned off. Current mobile application aims reduce significantly latency delays in reporting incidents in the university campus, thus providing victims the opportunity to receive timely assistance, facing their problems, and reduce the crime rate in and around the proposed smart campus. Concretely, the most important challenge the adopted system face is to find the real-time location of a victim in a smart campus building. In addition, many existing tracking systems are useless for capturing location in indoor environments, which results in inconvenient use or inaccurate solutions to pin point students' positions inside smart campus buildings. To overcome this inefficiency, proposed surveillance system uses the potentiality of existing wireless network capabilities to implement an indoor positioning algorithm able to provide student's fingerprint. Such algorithm is able to find on real time the position of students that facing a certain problem, through their smartphones' GPS signal. Subsequently, it is proposed a fine-grained location-aware smart campus surveillance safety system, which leverages hybrid positioning approaches with minimum deployment cost by incorporating Wi-Fi fingerprint enhanced with Bluetooth beacon technology. Such solution improves position accuracy to meter level with low implementation and maintenance costs.

Experiments with real data conducted in the campus where it is evaluated the proposed fine-grained location-aware security system. Results indicate that the adopted hybrid system incorporates efficiently the Wi-Fi fingerprint location approach and improves location accuracy with low cost. Scalability of the system in more areas in the campus as well as the limited adoption of the solution by student population are issues that should be fixed. Overall, it is a novel work that has high location accuracy; however, methods for the system to be adopted by the university community should be further examined.

In [82], the researchers present a mutual authentication protocol exploiting mobile RFID sensor technology to provide smart campus surveillance services. Specifically, an IoT platform is adopted to assist active monitoring, enhanced with surveillance cameras. The adopted surveillance system design is ad hoc and exploits social and movement user context. The supervised inference algorithms run on desktop and mobile applications and are able to capture abnormal students' activity. Authentication mechanisms and intrusion detection systems, which assure user privacy, are adopted to provide an integrated security solution. DoS, MTM, and data leakage attacks are efficiently prevented by the system with the incorporation of anonymization, data encryption, biometrics, and network monitoring mechanisms. A qualitative research methodology is followed, and the acquisition time of the research data is defined. Synthetic and batch text data sources are used for research experimentation.

Specifically, proposed system is based on mobile RFID technology, which can distinguish certain goals and read corresponding data through the radio signal. Intuitively, this system reads and writes the relevant transmitted data without physical contact. Adopted surveillance system exploits the three sections of mobile RFID technology, which are (1) the mobile reader, (2) tags, and (3) back-end knowledge base system. Concretely, the tag contains the product details and confident data for secure communications. In addition, the mobile reader provides a wireless link between the tag and the backend knowledge base system. Such utility allows data to be read from the tag and transmitted wirelessly in the knowledge base system, which is dedicated to store and process data sources. Subsequently, it holds that mobile RFID systems use wireless communication line to achieve communication between the involved parts, which makes the mobile

RFID system to support better mobility services. However, due to the wireless communication these systems are more vulnerable to malicious attacks from malevolent users outside the adopted system. Intuitively, such system proposes a mutual authentication protocol for providing smart campus unobtrusive surveillance services, which aim to enhance system's safety and privacy while reducing label cost and improving system authentication performance. Subsequently, adopted security protocol is able to face a vast number of malevolent situations by exploiting its components potentiality in the university campus safety framework. In addition, robust behavior of the system is of high significance in enhancing specific interoperable countermeasure functions of digital campus efficiency. Concretely, safety campus design and analysis are based on the following three aspects: (1) data security emerged issues, (2) personal privacy upcoming issues, and (3) illegal use of the system by malicious third parties. Adopted monitoring smart campus system is able to treat unobtrusively such potential safety categories.

Experiments are based on synthetic data used to improve existing mutual authentication protocol in mobile RFID card technology for smart campus. The experimental results are promising and the proposed system appears to lead to a strong, reliable, and effective security mechanism. Current research is tested only on synthetic data, thus there is a need to develop a new version that will be evaluated with real data as well. Overall, it is a well-defined mutual authentication approach for mobile RFID technology; however, more experiments with real data required.

The researchers in [83] propose a surveillance system for smart campus that focuses on data storage security, by incorporating a steganography security mechanism. The system aims at developing a cloud-based security architecture for efficient surveillance in the university campus. Specifically, an IoT platform, WSN and sensor technology, is adopted, while Wi-Fi wireless data communication for passive monitoring is incorporated in the solution. Active monitoring is based mainly on the use of cameras located in the campus. The surveillance system design is ad hoc and evaluates cloud-computing potentiality to process social user context. The system adopts mobile application technology. An intrusion detection system and an authentication system are incorporated to preserve students' security and privacy. Cryptanalysis, eavesdropping, and jamming attacks are prevented by the adoption of a steganography security mechanism. This effort is based on a quantitative research method. The data used for the experiments are from synthetic and streaming data sources, and the supported data types cover text and images.

Specifically, adopted unobtrusive surveillance smart campus system combines cloud computing and IoT technologies. A system architecture is defined, which incorporates (1) a user architecture, (2) smart university data and application center, and (3) sensor devices. Intuitively, user application provides a user-friendly GUI to support smart campus actors, like (1) students, (2) academics, (3) university personnel, and (4) general affair users. User application is responsible to interact with the smart campus application center on behalf of the endpoint users to provide them insight to the system as well as sufficient support. Concretely, university campus data and application center is responsible to provide the following services to users, such as (1) authentication service, (2) computation capabilities of the provided data sources, (3) control of the system to protect users from malicious attacks, (4) analysis of the stored data to assess meaningful information to understand current system's situation in the adopted infrastructure, and (5) visualization of the analyzed results to be easily observed by system administrator and campus control center. Subsequently, data and application center of the university campus has access and control to certain areas of activity, like (1) unified campus portal services, (2) service support center, (3) data integration platform, (4) network integration services platform, (5) standard information system security, and (6) maintenance system processes. In addition, sensor devices' component contains adopted technology for supporting the system. Such component interface consists of certain devices, such as (1) RFID sensors, (2) IoT sensors and actuators, and (3) network technologies. Concretely, proposed architecture supports a smart campus model, which is composed of three separate layers: (1) infrastructure layer, (2) supported services layer, and (3) software portal for decision support. Infrastructure layer contains network and hardware equipment as well as communication and sensor technologies. Supported services layer supports the following structural areas, such as (1) smart education and research, (2) smart resource and process management, (3) smart infrastructure sustainability and environment management, and (4) smart safety and security. Subsequently, smart campus portal is responsible for processing certain management services and providing decision support utilities to end users.

Experiments are based on synthetic data in the area of a cloud-computing testbed exploiting IoT technology. The main results are promising for the application of the proposed cloud-computing architecture to real campus environment. A limitation of this research effort is that the system is currently in development phase, and thus, its overall feasibility cannot be assessed. Overall, it is a cloud-computing architecture that combines high importance IoT potentiality, for smart campus surveillance; however, a deployment of the system in real environment is missing.

In [84], the authors introduce a surveillance system for smart campus based on signal strength maps. A prediction framework is developed, which incorporates random forests, to improve signal strength maps from limited measures. The core IoT enabling technology used in the research effort are sensor devices. Specifically, GPS sensor equipment enhanced with 5G communication technology is used for passive monitoring. Active monitoring is achieved through the incorporation of students' smartphones. The surveillance system design is mobile supported by cloud computing. Movement, crowdsourcing, and crowd sensing user context are all evaluated by the proposed system to provide a DSS for inferring abnormal student behavior. In addition, efficient supervised and semi-supervised machine learning algorithms are used for activity recognition. An intrusion detection system is introduced, and spoofing attacks are prevented by the incorporation of a password authentication mechanism. The research method followed in this effort is quantitative. Experiments are based on real and streaming data, and the system supports text data sources.

Specifically, proposed smart campus system incorporates cellular providers' key performance indicators (KPIs) to investigate the performance and signal coverage of the supported campus network. KPIs focus on wireless channel measurements and other performance metrics, like (1) throughput, (2) delay, (3) frequency band, (4) spatial context, and (5) temporal context. Concretely, adopted signal maps contain certain number of measurements of associated KPIs, which are of significant importance to wireless network operators regarding: (1) network management, (2) system maintenance, (3) network software updates, (4) service operations, and (5) infrastructure troubleshooting. University campus network cellular providers are able to collect data measurements at the edge of the network and further outsourced the produced data sets to third parties for further network data analytical processing. Such smart campus analysis is based on certain administration parameters, like (1) cost, (2) liability of privacy end user context, (3) limited access to other networks. Intuitively, mobile data analytics industrial partners incorporate crowdsourcing methods to exploit data patterns produced from end-user devices through a specific smartphone mobile application. Subsequently, large scale of university campus signal map collection is feasible due to a decentralized edge network infrastructure. However, measurements are possible to be sparse in space, which is related to end-users' position in the university campus area. In addition, such measurements could also be sparse in temporal dimension, which is possible in case they are collected infrequently. In each case, signal strength manipulation of the whole university campus' maps is expensive to be performed by the campus administration control center, thus it is assigned to third-party companies, which incorporate crowdsourcing models to achieve their goals. Proposed unobtrusive surveillance system is designed to improve the trade-off between cost of measurements and observed quality with regards to system coverage and accuracy evaluation metrics. Concretely, signal maps are produced through signal strength spatiotemporal positioning from limited university campus generated measurements. A machine learning model is proposed to handle multiple features of observed signal strength measurements, which is based on random forest classification algorithm. Intuitively, such machine learning model incorporates (1) spatial location, (2) temporal dimension, (3) cell identifier, (4) device hardware information, (5) distance from the wireless network antenna, (6) observed frequency band, and (7) indoor and outdoor position of the receiver that affects the wireless network precision.

The experiments are performed in a laboratory with real data provided by participants. Results prove that the proposed system can significantly improve the trade-off between prediction error and appropriate number of measurements required. Laboratory experimental setup is a limitation of the considered study. Specifically, incorporating data provided from more areas of the smart campus should do scaling of the system. Overall, the system achieves efficient prediction accuracy; however, scaling of the research work is a need to evaluate the system in the whole area of the campus.

In [85], the researchers present a context-aware authentication framework, using students' information available is the smart campus. The developed authentication framework can be the basis for the development of certain mobile context-aware services. Specifically, the proposed system incorporates smart traffic lights from the physical infrastructure. In addition, an IoT platform is adopted, which handles data produced by connected sensors, such as RFID and GPS sensors. These sensors communicate through Wi-Fi, Bluetooth, and NFC wireless data communication protocols, while cameras and users' smartphones achieve active monitoring. The surveillance system design is ad hoc. The user social activity and movement is inserted into a context-aware system. The service-oriented architecture adopted to provide the capability of supervised inference algorithms, and the system incorporates mobile applications. An authentication system and an intrusion detection system are proposed to preserve security goals and comply with certain security standards. Sniffing attacks are prevented by the adoption of efficient data encryption and password mechanisms. This effort is based on a quantitative research method. The data used for experiments derive from real and batch image data sources.

Specifically, adopted university campus system proposes a context-aware authentication framework. Such framework is based on the discretization of the automated actions performed by the system and the actions performed explicitly by the users to achieve authentication service. A lightweight mechanism is incorporated, which is able to capture user's action on real time through QR codes, which are defined as a two-dimensional barcode. Proposed campus system has certain strengths in implementation and deployment compared with other access control systems. Concretely, QR codes are easier to generate while they can be read by almost all smartphones' cameras. In addition, such technology is robust against sniffing attacks, which compromise any other radio-based tags such as RFID. Adopted smart campus system further combines user roles with location-based access control processes to enhance observed context to allow the definition of certain rules, which are based on both the user roles and current positioning. Subsequently, there is proposed a specific set of policies implemented by the adopted university surveillance system, which facilitates its decision-making process. Intuitively, decision-making capability is based on the user's roles and certain position attempted to access. A certain scenario is provided to understand the proposed system in more depth. Actually, it is described a common daily activity of a student into the campus as well as the access control process, which is based on QR code infrastructure. Concretely, student's private information is registered to the system with the adoption of a dedicated server, which is managed by the smart campus control center. Student's private information includes (1) identification number, (2) name, (3) e-mail, (4) username, (5) academic track, (6) spatiotemporal context of daily activity in the campus, (7) meeting times, and (8) usual arrival time to the campus. QR codes are presented on various monitors in the university campus, where the student can scan the assigned QR code with the smartphone. Upon QR code scanning, student receives a web link on the smartphone, which allows the student to use campus Wi-Fi and other infrastructure utilities. Intuitively, this is allowed since student's information is verified by the system's server to provide student a pleasant access to university campus' resources.

Laboratory experiments based on real data provided mainly by soft sensors and other IoT equipment is the core of the evaluation schema. Results present an extensible context-aware authentication system which is able to adopt contextual information available in the university campus environment. The system should scale up to more places in the campus rather than only focusing on smart buildings and public spaces. This is an interesting research effort that lacks large-scale deployment.

The authors in [86] introduce a flexible smart campus surveillance system, which is based on service-oriented architecture, to support social behavior in a university campus environment. A mobile middleware able to process social context is designed in the client frontend. In the server backend, context is aggregated and analyzed to facilitate social interactions. Specifically, the proposed system leverages IoT platform and sensor technologies. Passive monitoring is achieved through the incorporation of GPS sensors, and Ethernet, Wi-Fi, and Bluetooth communication protocols. Active monitoring is supported by the adoption of students' smartphone devices. The surveillance system design is mobile and exploits both social context and movement of the user to support a service-oriented architecture. A DSS is designed to infer a possible student abnormal behavior incident based on supervised and unsupervised machine learning algorithms. The suggested system incorporates mobile applications. An authentication system is used according to security standards. Sniffing attacks are prevented by the adoption of efficient biometrics and network monitoring security mechanisms. A quantitative research methodology is adopted, and the acquisition time of research completion is defined. The textual data used for experimentation are from real and streaming data sources.

Specifically, proposed unobtrusive surveillance smart campus system is based on mobile social network (MSN) capabilities. Intuitively, an MSN is able to provide continuous seamless sensing, which allows university campus control center to obtain specific contexts from physical world entities. A plethora of different contexts may be extracted from IoT sensors embedded in smartphone devices. Mobility feasibility of MSN produce several data sources annotated with spatiotemporal context. Such meaningful context provides in depth knowledge in every user activity and social behavior. In addition, MSN enables the possibility of egocentric services' emergence incorporating groups of users acting locally anywhere and at any time in the university campus area. Such feature of MSN technology is able to enhance users' personal and social experience. Subsequently, MSN are enhanced with the support of social interactions in the real world, which make them able to exploit full use of smartphones' potentiality. Such feature is able to extract social contexts by analyzing sensing data, which are provided by engaged social services. Proposed system is based on a flexible mobile social networking architecture, which exploits service-oriented perspective to support certain social interactions. Concretely, in the client side a mobile middleware is incorporated for social context collection, such as proximity and communication history. Server side is responsible to aggregate transmitted contexts, perform data analysis of the social connections between user groups and providing specific social services to enable social interaction. In addition, based on the adopted smart campus system architecture, there are implemented certain applications, which are available to end users. Furthermore, proposed system requirements include (1) semantic extraction, (2) pattern mining, (3) ubiquitous search, (4) location management, (5) scalability potentiality, (6) lightweight infrastructure, and (7) connectivity among several devices.

Experiments exploit real data and elaborate a flexible system architecture based on detailed service-oriented specification to support social interaction in university campus. Results prove that the designed mobile middleware can collect social context to provide surveillance service on campus environment. The system runs on a prototype deployed only on smart buildings and public places. Overall, it is a solid work with appropriate experimental testing; however, it should be expanded to the whole university campus environment.

In [87], the researcher presents a surveillance system subject to a spatiotemporal authentication method. The system generates a unique identifier for use in authentication, by adopting context-aware student's data, during actual presence in the smart campus. Particularly, the system adopts an IoT platform, WSN, sensors, and actuators technologies. Passive monitoring is based on RFID and GPS sensors and on Ethernet, Wi-Fi, NFC, and 5G data communication protocols. Active monitoring devices include cameras and ATM located in the university campus. The surveillance system design is mesh, combining ad hoc and mobile components, and the movement and crowd sensing user context are processed in the cloud. A big data architecture is used, which inserts data into a context-aware system, for inferring abnormal student behavior. Inference is based on supervised and unsupervised algorithms, and the system incorporates desktop applications. An authentication system is proposed to fulfill students' security and privacy requirements, and incorporates data encryption, biometrics, and network monitoring security mechanisms. Adopted research is based on a quantitative research methodology, and experimentation data include real and streaming data. The supported data types are from text, image and video data sources.

Specifically, adopted smart campus system is based on a method, which generates a unique identifier for further use in the authentication process. Concretely, such unique identifier is generated from context-awareness technology, which is composed of (1) spatiotemporal history, (2) facial recognition, (3) gesture recognition, (4) voice recognition, and (5) emotion recognition of a university campus user. Authentication process is required to provide accessed to (1) a particular location in the campus and (2) a sensitive information stored on a smart campus computer system. In addition, authentication process is also required to allow a user to perform a particular action such as to make a bank transfer. Proposed monitoring system, address the previous problems by providing an authentication method that incorporates users' context-awareness, which has been measured using third parties' systems such as CCTV networks, automated teller machine (ATM) networks, and electronic pass networks. Such gathered information is used to determine a context-aware fingerprint, which is unique to each user. Intuitively, the unique identifier is not derived from a single device carried by the individual, but instead is derived by fusion of data from multiple sources with which the user interacts through daily activity in the university campus. This fingerprint can be further used to verify a user as well as to detect a malicious and unexpected behavior.

Experimental setup exploits real data provided for laboratory test purposes. Results provide a spatiotemporal authentication system, which is based on users' movement data collected on the smart campus. A limitation of the adopted effort is that the system evaluates only data captured by limited data sources. Overall, it is an interesting research work toward the definition of a spatiotemporal authentication scheme in university campus; however, more data sources should be incorporated to evaluate the research effort.

The researcher in [88] proposes an extension of the surveillance system introduced in [67] to provide a more robust and integrated context-aware spatiotemporal authentication method for smart campus adoption. To avoid duplications, we present only these components and features, which are not listed in the previous research effort since this effort is a superset of the prior one. Specifically, the proposed system adopts UAV and connected and autonomous vehicle (CAV) technologies as part of the physical surveillance infrastructure. The system differs from the previous one because it takes into consideration as well microphones and smartphones as part of the active monitoring components. It extends adopted inference algorithms by using semi-supervised machine learning algorithms, as well as mobile applications. Regarding experimental data, it uses additional sound data sources.

Specifically, proposed unobtrusive surveillance smart campus system incorporates the potentiality of a method, which is able to generate a unique identifier for authentication usage. Such unique identifier is generated from students' context-awareness information, which is composed of: (1) spatiotemporal stochastic behavior, (2) facial recognition, (3) gesture recognition, (4) voice recognition, and (5) emotion recognition of certain student. Authentication process is required to provide access to a particular position in the smart campus or to gain access to sensitive information of a student stored on a server. In addition, authentication component of the adopted system is able to allow a student to perform a certain action, like to make a bank withdrawal. Context-awareness is incorporated to exploit user information, which has been measured using third-party surveillance systems. Such systems include CCTV networks, microphone networks, UAV networks, CAV networks, ATM networks, electronic pass networks, which are used to determine the contextual information fingerprint that is unique to a certain student. Concretely, unique identifier is not derived from a single device carried by the student. Instead fingerprint is produced by an amalgamation of data captured from multiple third-party systems with which the student interacts during daily activity. Intuitively, such unique fingerprint can be further used to verify a student and detect malevolent, abnormal and unexpected possible future students' behavior.

Experimental setup is based on real data captured from certain areas of the university campus. Results provide a spatiotemporal authentication schema, which is based on users' spatiotemporal history data as well as biometric recognition data sources. A limitation of current effort is that there is a need for data sources provided by robots moving in the smart campus environment. Broadly, a solid work, which provides spatiotemporal authentication as part of an integrated smart campus surveillance system, however robots should be used to explore areas that other devices cannot reach. Future work is required to observe better results of the proposed systems in the area of smart campus surveillance systems. Specifically, more work it required, in [80], toward an extension of current research toward gesture recognition detection for surveillance in campus. More work should be performed, in [81], focusing on the addition of more single techniques to enhance the proposed hybrid localization system. Extensive work, in [82], should focus on the application of the proposed authentication protocol to a wider area of the campus extending smart buildings and public spaces. Future directions, in [83], should focus on the development of appropriate software, which will improve security of the campus cloud resources. More work is required, in [84], which should include a hybrid machine learning propagation model to optimize current research schema. Contemporary work, in [85], should focus on fingerprinting context as well as of using cues from users' stochastic history to define unique user profiling for authentication purposes. Future research work, in [86], should focus on exploiting stochastic social interactions captured by the system to provide extensive authentication services. More work, in [87], should take into consideration online data sources provided by CAV and UAV as part of an integrated surveillance system. Future work, in [88], should focus on how CAV, UAV, and robotic data will be fused to infer and provide an integrated surveillance system for the purposes of smart campus.

5.9 Systems That Focus on Smart Campus Ambient Intelligence and User Context

In [89–94], researchers propose surveillance systems that focus on smart campus Ambient Intelligence (AmI) user context. Specifically, in [89], the authors propose a surveillance system for smart campus, which focuses in smart labs and public spaces. Proposed system incorporates an IoT platform, which exploits sensors and WSN potentiality. Passive monitoring is based on RFID and Ethernet technology, while active monitoring is achieved by the use of cameras installed in the smart campus. Surveillance system design is based on mobile technology, while computing methodology adopted is cloud computing. It is used face recognition to enhance the operability of the system, while user-context support is focusing in user movement and AmI. Service-oriented software architecture is proposed, while inference system exploits context-aware potentiality. Inference algorithms are based on supervised classification models, while VR capabilities are also supported. System runs in both desktop and mobile application environments. An intrusion detection system is used to support security standards. Security standards are exploiting network monitoring potentiality. Acquisition time to complete the research is mentioned, while the effort is using mixed research methodology. Data context incorporating includes real text data as well as images and video data sources.

Specifically, adopted monitoring smart campus system is based on IoT technology enhanced with edge-computing and AmI potentiality for providing event-driven video services. Such services are used for surveillance purposes at the university campus environments. IoT devices enable development and implementation of certain digital services at the campus. Subsequently, edge-centric and fog-computing technologies are able to provide added value to IoT infrastructure with regards to specific monitoring services. Concretely, video services can detect complex events based on semantic linking between the observed events and the provided context from the existing IoT framework. Data analysis could be performed locally by exploiting edge-computing technology as well as smart campus video analytics, which are performed by dedicated agents able to infer a possible malicious user behavior. Intuitively, proposed system is able to manipulate certain conceptual classes of contemporary video service processing, which are implemented by the edge-centric IoT infrastructure. Concretely, key component features of the adopted service responsible for emergence of video streaming conceptual classes are (1) microservice-based system for operating with specific multiple data sources, (2) an event-driven model for certain service construction, and (3) context-based mechanisms for further use in video data analytics. A conceptual model is analyzed and certain results are presented, which is based on an event-driven context-based model for local video data streaming processing. In addition, proposed unobtrusive surveillance smart campus system is enhanced with an implemented and deployed video service, which is incorporated for the university personnel recognition around a certain campus area. Such video service is feasible due to dedicated cameras able to provide various types of services, like (1) informational service, which informing the system about an upcoming event is the university, (2) analytical service, which provides the opportunity to review and analyze the data leading to certain event, and (3) recommendation service, which predict on real time the occurrence of an event enabling the user to make certain alternative actions with existing equipment. Intuitively, such services are further used in digital monitoring and smart early warning and prediction process in case of malevolent attack to the adopted system. Subsequently, certain cameras are located in specific areas of the smart campus to track various activities performed by students, faculty members and university personnel.

Experimental setup is based on real data captured from smart campus labs and public spaces. Results indicate an intrusion detection system, which is based on network monitoring. A limitation of the adopted effort is that it should incorporate more security mechanisms to provide a safer surveillance environment. Overall, it is an interesting research effort, which provides surveillance utilities based on an intrusion detection system; however, a list of attacks it faces should be listed in more detail.

The researchers in [90] propose a surveillance system for university campus, which focuses on smart buildings, smart classes, public spaces and smart lighting. Adopted system uses IoT technology exploiting WSN, and sensors and actuators capabilities. Passive monitoring is achieved through GPS, Wi-Fi, Bluetooth, and ZigBee connectivity. Active monitoring is based on cameras and smartphones. Surveillance system design exploits mobile potentiality, while computing methodology incorporates cloud computing. Social, movement, and AmI user context is processed, while software architecture is service-oriented. Inference system incorporates context-aware techniques, while inference algorithms used exploit semi-supervised models' capabilities. Proposed system uses VR interfaces, while it is executed on mobile application environment. An intrusion detection system is elaborated to provide anonymization and network monitoring security mechanisms operability. Acquisition time required to complete current effort is provided, while research is based on quantitative methodology. Real streaming data sources are incorporated exploited text, image, and video data types.

Specifically, proposed smart surveillance system is designed to provide students' valuable assistance during their daily activities in the university campus. Emergence of monitoring smart campus capabilities are explained due to certain strengths observed in the area of IoT and AmI technological advancements. Subsequently, contemporary computing environments are enhanced by the incorporation of digital networked devices, such as sensors and actuators embedded in smart campus indoor and outdoor coverage areas. These devices are able to sense students' activities and forward such information to the university campus control center for further examination. Such system properties are based on the capabilities IoT-enabled devices have due to their connectivity to the internet. Concretely, it is possible these spatially limited devices to be interconnected, thus forming a computational grid, which is able to surround human activities in several university campus areas. Intuitively, physical world is transformed to digital cyber space, which enables connectivity of emerged data sources. Such smart environments are equipped with adequate software applications to provide a context-aware system infrastructure. Concretely, observed data are manipulated computationally to provide rich information at the edge of the network, which is associated with certain semantics collected in the university campus spaces. Such semantics are further explored to result into specific ontological representation models available on the semantic web. Intuitively, ontological models form a knowledge base able to provide and support interoperability services among students, academics, and smart campus personnel. Designing a smart surveillance system infrastructure is a complicated goal, which requires a formal point of view incorporating certain middleware, basic software engineering architecture knowledge, stochastic vision, and programming primitives for development as well as implementation of specific software applications. In addition, developed smart campus monitoring system could fuse data sources perceived from both physical and digital worlds, which should be manipulated approximately to serve upcoming users' needs.

Experiments are based on real streaming data produced in smart campus' buildings, classes, public spaces, and smart lighting infrastructure. Results prove that the adopted surveillance system is able to efficiently monitor network data traffic. A limitation of the proposed system is that it does not declare possible types of attacks it treats. Overall, it is an interesting research work, which provides surveillance capabilities incorporating AmI user context; however, a more detailed list of security standards used should also be mentioned.

In [91], the researchers present a surveillance system, which is focusing on providing safety services to smart campus' building, classes, public spaces, and smart parking physical infrastructure. Proposed research effort also incorporates electric vehicle technology, while adopted IoT platform exploits sensors' potentiality. Passive monitoring technology incorporates Bluetooth connectivity among mobile surveillance devices, while active monitoring is based on security cameras. Surveillance system supported is mobile, while computing methodology is focused on edge-computing techniques. Social and AmI user context is analyzed, while a service-oriented software architecture is used. Adopted context-aware inference system enhances the capabilities of incorporated supervised inference algorithms, which are running on mobile application environments. Proposed authentication cyber security system complies with security standards and privacy regulations. Security system is able to face DoS attacks by incorporating network monitoring safety mechanisms. Acquisition time of research is mentioned, while it is adopted quantitative methodology. Research effort exploits real streaming video data sources.

Specifically, adopted monitoring sustainable smart campus safety system is based on a context-aware service platform, which is able to exchange and share context in an IoT and AmI smart ecosystem. Concretely, context-awareness is a core area of IoT technology, which evolves the requirements for accessing contextual information online and in real time. Such requirements have become a significant factor for the IoT-enabled services aiming to add certain value in the surveillance university campus system's architecture. Consequently, a middleware platform could be possible to be built, which would manage interactions with sources of students' daily activities concept to provide specific contextual information to assisting context-aware software applications as an integrated service. Proposed surveillance smart campus safety system is based on a context management platform, which enables software applications to provide and consume students' context captured in the university coverage area seamlessly without requiring supplementary computational effort. A distinguished feature of the adopted system is the incorporation of certain abstract context requests, which serve the proposed model and support high-level context querying to the associated knowledge base. Such technical support enables advanced context-aware services with regards to terms of semantic signature, service's special characteristics as well as certain contextual behavior's specification. Intuitively, proposed reference architecture is implemented and demonstrated for smart campus monitoring safety system's purposes to exemplify the required context-aware service. Such service is able to exploit IoT infrastructure potentiality to utilize and retrieve adequate information based on emerged data sources from campus area distributed and embedded devices.

Experiments are based on real streaming data captured from smart campus physical infrastructure. Results indicate that the adopted surveillance system complies with certain security standards and privacy regulations. A limitation of the proposed effort is the rather limited amount of data sources used to provide early warning surveillance services. Overall, it is a precise research work, which provides decent surveillance results; however, more experiments should be performed by incorporating more precise data sources.

The authors in [92] present a smart campus surveillance system, which faces inefficiencies in smart buildings, smart labs, public spaces, and smart lighting infrastructure. Proposed system incorporates an IoT platform exploiting sensors capabilities. Passive monitoring devices contain GPS technology, while active monitoring is mainly based on cameras installed in the university campus infrastructure. Surveillance system design is ad hoc, while adopted system exploits edge-computing potentiality. Social, crowd sensing, and AmI user context is exploited. Software architecture is based on big data, while it is used as a decision support inference system. Classification algorithms enhance the inference process of the proposed system, while there are elaborated mobile applications to test and evaluate the system. Cyber security system is based on intrusion detection mechanisms, while security standards are incorporated. Password capture attacks are faced with the incorporation of data encryption, network monitoring, and password policy security mechanisms. Time required to conduct the research is mentioned, while the type of the research is mixed incorporating quantitative and qualitative methodology. Data context used is based on real text data sources.

Specifically, proposed unobtrusive monitoring smart campus safety system is based on existing IoT technology to create a scalable university campus living laboratory, which is able to promote energy savings and green ecosystem sustainability. Such environment exploits emerged challenges and opportunities in AmI-enabled developing smart campus buildings and public spaces. Consequently, certain analyzed data sources provided by the existing design of the building management system is able to be further processed by a specific integrated service analysis and optimization software design phase. Such analysis aims to identify several opportunities for sustainable system innovation with regards to certain constrains, which also focus on specific challenges that enable proposed system's viability. Subsequently, multibuilding campuses may span both of their class and laboratory spaces is sparse smart campus areas, which results in densely populated places where students conduct a multitude of their daily practices. Provided resources and IoT infrastructure of such campuses are directly linked to the physical world space of the university campus. In addition, software developers are possible to face technical and organizational barriers involving complicated financial and institutional constraints based on certain underlying system functional priorities. Concretely, smart campus living laboratory is able to integrate experimental safety control along with on-demand AmI-based technologies, which enable smart campus surveillance purposes to track malevolent user behavior. Intuitively, adopted system incorporates several software decision support inference models to understand students' roles and activities in the university campus as well as how this piece of information relates to campus safety process. Furthermore, it is also important to be able to understand the implications of smart campuses along with included living laboratories by monitoring students' behavior who live, work, and study within them.

Experimental setup exploits real text data sources captured from the university campus infrastructure. Results toward an efficient intrusion detection system are promising. A limitation of the proposed research effort is that it is based only of text data sources. Overall it is a solid surveillance system work; however, more rich data sources should be incorporated to enhance potentiality of current system.

In [93], the authors propose a surveillance system, which provides unobtrusive monitoring to public spaces and smart traffic lights of a university campus. Adopted system also incorporates UAV technology for achieving high quality of supported surveillance in the smart campus. An IoT platform is used to enhance the efficiency of the system along with WSN and sensors capabilities. Passive monitory is based on GPS technology, while active monitoring is achieved through installed cameras in the campus infrastructure. It is supported a mobile surveillance system design, while cloud-computing potentiality is exploited. System incorporates face recognition techniques, while user context is based on crowdsourcing, crowd sensing, and AmI technologies. Software architecture incorporates big data design, while it is used a decision support inference system, which exploits unsupervised and semi-supervised inference algorithms. Adopted system application is running in both desktop and mobile environments. Cyber security is preserved with an authentication system. Security standards and privacy compliance regulations are supported by the proposed system, while it is incorporated a network monitoring mechanism to treat upcoming attacks. Research methodology is mixed, while time span of the effort is defined. Data used are real and synthetic, while there are also incorporated streaming, image, and video data sources.

Specifically, adopted surveillance safety smart campus system incorporates IoT cameras to enable single student and crowd data sources' analysis, which is based on an augmentation model for automatic students' activity detection for further exploitation. Consequently, provided system enables video monitoring over heterogeneous networks to achieve a certain level of security, which is of high importance in a smart campus environment where students' and crowd behavior is observed. Subsequently, crowd detection and behavior recognition are based on video processing with several computer vision approaches, such as machine learning inference models. Results observed by such models can be further improved by providing label data, which achieve less computation costs and higher students' behavior prediction accuracy. Adopted system is first trained on synthetic data sources, which are initialized from real world users' movement in the university campus. In addition, to increase system's efficiency synthetic labeled data are adjusted to the inference model by sing real data sources. Such data collections can be used to differentiate contextual information between a single student and a group of students' behaviors. Concretely, proposed system extends prior research in the area by incorporating several IoT cameras potentiality in the smart campus. Such technology enables 3D spatiotemporal monitoring in real-time video sequences, which have the ability to affect the obtained model's effectiveness. In addition, surveillance system adopted for assuring safety in the university campus also exploits a proposed AmI framework technology, which supports multiple cameras to track moving users' targets and generate appropriate 3D videos instead of limited value single images. Such technology is based on a certain compositing technique, which is used to generate realistic videos by superimposing virtual objects in real scenes. Intuitively, such technique is able to reduce the complexity of single student as well as crowd students' computation cost while further focusing on accurate position estimation and student tracking.

Experiments are based on both real and synthetic online data streaming. Results indicating the importance of a smart campus dedicated surveillance system are well presented. A limitation of the presented research effort is that security mechanisms are only based on network monitoring, while there are a lot of other mechanisms to enhance cyber security system efficiency. Overall it is a well-structured work; however, more advanced security mechanisms are needed to support the proposed research effort.

The researchers in [94] present a university campus surveillance system, which focuses on smart buildings, smart classes, smart parking, and smart lighting. Proposed system also adopts smart traffic lights surveillance capabilities. IoT technology is incorporated along with WSN and sensors potentiality. Passive monitoring technology is achieved by RFID, Wi-Fi, Bluetooth, ZigBee, and NFC supported equipment, while cameras are used for active monitoring. Surveillance system design is mobile, while computing methodology is based on cloud technology. User context is based on crowd sensing and AmI, while software architecture is service-oriented. Inference system is context aware, while the inference algorithms are based on supervised, unsupervised, and semi-supervised techniques. Extended reality (XR) capabilities are based on VR technology, while the system runs on a mobile application environment. It is adopted an authentication cyber security system, while the surveillance technology incorporates security standards. Password capture and virus infection attacks are faced with the incorporation of network monitoring and antivirus system security mechanisms. Acquisition time of the effort is defined, while research methodology used is quantitative. Data context is composed of real streaming data, while there are also used image and video data sources.

Specifically, proposed unobtrusive surveillance smart campus safety system exploits edge computing, AmI and IoT technologies potentiality to provide integrated university campus services. Such services are provided with regards to extensive network data analysis from observed campus users, like students, academics, and university personnel. IoT technology is perceived as an assisting component for enabling teaching environment capabilities, which include several services such as virtual classrooms, online learning utilities, and shared laboratories located in sparse places within the university campus. In addition, IoT devices such as sensors and actuators located in the smart campus are able to provide campus monitoring safety, environmental awareness, and sustainable energy management. Concretely, excessive campus resources exploit cloud environment potentiality, which has also a certain impact on the learning and working university processes. Intuitively, campus environment is able to manage effectively different innovative applications. However, such technical innovative software applications require excessive computational power and emerged costs. Subsequently, execution of an IoT campus application such as students' monitoring, online courses, and shared laboratories require cloud resources, which are provided be the dedicated campus server. In addition, adopted smart campus environment is able to face certain technical issues such as university security, adopted campus allocation balance, and increased energy consumption. Concretely, in cases where there exist several IoT devices transmitting continuously produced data sources, timing of digital network environment is affected thus assigned software tasks observe low QoS. To overcome such ineffectiveness, adopted system incorporates a decentralized edge-computing platform, which is able to treat efficiently emerged network latencies, thus providing accurate and in real time system responses to certain software requests. Subsequently, such framework is able to treat online resource allocation requirements and to provide effective smart campus monitoring services.

Experimental setup is based on real streaming data sources produced from the smart campus area. Results are encouraging in adopting a well-defined surveillance system. A limitation of the effort is that it uses only cameras as an active monitoring technology. Overall, it is a compact research effort in the area of university campus surveillance systems, however more active monitoring devices should be adopted to enhance the efficiency of the system.

Based on the observed results, it is obvious that significant work should be done. Specifically, in [89], future work should include a detailed list of upcoming attacks the system handles to provide a safer infrastructure. Further analysis of attacks faced by proposed system, in [90], should be listed in more detail. More experimentation is needed, in [91], with incorporating more precise data sources. Further research work is required in, [92], establishing a robust surveillance system, which will use multiple data sources to unobtrusively detect anomalies in the smart campus infrastructure. Further use of more security mechanisms are required, in [93], to enhance the potentiality of the proposed surveillance system. Further work is required, in [94], to support a more robust system by incorporating a variety of active monitoring technology devices.

5.10 Systems That Focus on Smart Campus Low-Power Wide Area Networks Technology

In [95–101], researchers propose surveillance systems that focus on smart campus low-power wireless area network (LPWAN) technology. Specifically, in [95] the authors propose a university campus surveillance system. Such system monitors unobtrusively students' behavioral context captured in smart buildings, public spaces, smart parking, and smart lighting infrastructure. Electric vehicles are also used as monitoring devices. Adopted system incorporates an IoT platform along with Raspberry Pi, Arduino Uno, WSN, sensors, and actuators devices. Passive monitoring is achieved with the incorporation of GPS, Ethernet, Wi-Fi, Bluetooth, and LPWAN technologies. Active monitoring is based on cameras installed in the smart campus infrastructure as well as students' smartphones. Surveillance system design is mobile, while it is supported cloud-computing methodology. Social and movement user context is evaluated, while software architecture is service-oriented. A decision support inference system is incorporated, while there are supported supervised inference algorithms. Proposed system is running on mobile application environment. An intrusion detection system, which preserves security, and privacy regulations is used to face hacking attacks. There are also incorporated anonymization, data encryption and network monitoring security mechanisms to treat malicious intruders' behavior. Time span of research conducted is declared, while qualitative research methodology is followed in the adopted effort. Real data context is used, while there are supported text, image, and video data sources.

Specifically, adopted unobtrusive surveillance smart campus safety system is based on an IoT-enabled platform, which is able to monitor online and in real-time students' movement trajectories in the university campus. In addition, proposed system is also able to monitor environmental pollution indicators as a QoS metric for the residents of the smart campus. Intuitively, sustainable development of smart campus is currently a major issue in contemporary academic invention and industrial innovation research. The main goal of smart campus is to provide a safe environment where the students will be able to evolve freely in learning activities, thus developing the next generation of academics and professionals. To achieve this goal, proposed system is focusing on designing, implementing, and deploying an IoT-based platform, which will aim to provide specific emphasis on several technological challenges. Such challenges will be faced during the period where adequate solutions will be adopted for assuring students' safety during their daily activities in the university campus. Subsequently, proposed system is able to evaluate in real time observed functionality of specific services, which will exploit the operational potentiality of the implemented IoT platform. Adopted platform should be designed optimally to be well aligned with certain system technical requirements, such as to be (1) of low computational cost, (2) scalable and easy to integrate with other existing smart campus systems, and (3) based on standardized and open-source software solutions. Consequently, such requirements will enable the incorporation of certain upcoming services including exploiting university campus surveillance potentiality for possible malevolent behavior, which might be observed by specific campus individuals. Concretely, adopted system architecture, which supports systems' operation is based on several software components able to be aligned with standards available to assure IoT and network engineering compatibility. Intuitively, proposed system architecture overview is based on certain layers, like (1) sensing layer that is composed by a set of sensors, (2) networking and data communication layer that represents the core IP-based communications infrastructure, and (3) the application layer where the service logic and algorithms reside.

Experiments are based on real online data sources. Results focus on a robust surveillance system adopted by a certain university campus. A limitation of the proposed research is that there are only used supervised inference algorithms. Overall it is a solid work; however, more precise inference algorithms and techniques should be incorporated in the presented research effort.

The researchers in [96] present a smart campus surveillance system, which is based on the monitoring of smart buildings, smart labs and smart traffic lights. Specifically, IoT technology is adopted, which incorporates WSN, sensors, and actuators devices. Passive monitoring is based on Wi-Fi, Bluetooth, 5G and LPWAN technologies. Active monitoring is mainly achieved with cameras, which are installed in the university campus area. Surveillance system design is mobile, while edge-computing methodology is adopted. Software architecture is service-oriented, while inference system is based on decision support models. Adopted system runs in both desktop and mobile application environments. An authentication cyber security system is incorporated, which confronts with security standards. Proposed system is able to face sniffing attacks by using data encryption and network monitoring security mechanisms. Acquisition time to conduct the research is mentioned, while research methodology followed is quantitative. Data context required by the adopted system incorporates text and image data sources.

Specifically, proposed monitoring smart campus safety system is based on IoT-devices and wireless area network technologies. Concretely, IoT technology involves deployment of sensors and actuators embedded in several smart campus areas. Intuitively, sensors are responsible to report captured data over a certain communication link, which facilitates university campus surveillance service capabilities.

Unobtrusive management applications are also incorporated in a variety of physical and digital domains in the campus. A specific feature of such system's architecture is the requirement that several devices should be able to consume a limited amount of electric power to continue operating using available battery power for many years. In addition, not every IoT software application require high data rate per certain online service operation. Consequently, a specific amount of IoT software applications are robust to delays and network latencies, thus being loss tolerant while they transmit data infrequently in time. Such applications require low-cost connectivity, which is motivated by the need for alternative solutions to bridge the gap between the short range and cellular-based alternative network approaches. Such technical requirements are treated optimally by incorporating LPWAN network technology, which is able to sufficiently bridge the existing communication gap between the short range and cellular-based networks' interoperability. The objective contribution of the adopted unobtrusive surveillance system is the optimal observed performance efficiency within the specific coverage area of the university campus. In addition, certain focus is also given to the observation and reporting of malevolent user activity, which impacts specific network transmission parameters' settings to keep proposed system stable to emergent user's behaviors.

Experimental setup is based mainly on text and image data sources. Results lead to a surveillance system, which exploits LPWAN technology to achieve unobtrusive monitoring. A limitation of the adopted work is that it is not described in detail either the user context or the algorithms used to infer a malicious behavior in the smart campus.

In [97], the researchers propose a surveillance system for university campus, which focuses on smart buildings, smart classes, and smart laboratories. An IoT platform along with WSN and sensor devices is also incorporated. Passive monitoring is using RFID, GPS, Bluetooth, 5G, and LPWAN technology, while active monitoring incorporates mainly surveillance cameras located in certain places within the smart campus infrastructure. Surveillance system design in based on mobile technology, while it is adopted cloud-computing methodology. There are also supported face recognition techniques along with social and movement user context. Big data software architecture is incorporated, while context-aware inference system potentiality is exploited. Proposed system is running on mobile application environment. Cyber security is based on an authentication system, which confronts with security and privacy regulations. Adopted system supports data encryption and network monitoring security mechanisms. Time span of the effort is mentioned, while research methodology used is mixed containing both quantitative and qualitative research. Data context is mainly online real streaming composed by sound, image, and video data sources.

Specifically, adopted unobtrusive surveillance university campus safety system is based on IoT and 5G network technologies. Concretely, proposed system exploits 5G network potentiality to construct a robust smart campus sustainable environment. Subsequently, special focus is provided to smartphone mobile application incorporated to support teaching in the adopted platform, which connects in real time both academics and students during the learning process. Such platform also aids to enrich students' online learning resources as well as improving academics' teaching performance. Smart campus construction is a complex process, which combines not certain actors' behavior and daily activities. Such actors are students, academics, and university personnel living and interacting within the smart campus. Surveillance services along with improvements in the education technology and processes are part of the adopted system to track users' behavior. Consequently, monitored students are able to sign-in during the teaching process in the class rooms and the laboratories. Such online monitoring is feasible due to 5G network technology along with dedicated mobile terminals to achieve an efficient system performance. Proposed system enables a framework, which is based on certain technical improvements, like (1) IoT technology able to transmit data in continuous rates at the transport layer and (2) 5G network connectivity and computational capabilities. Intuitively, adopted IoT framework enables smart campus interoperability based on certain infrastructure layers, such as (1) perception layer, (2) network layer, (3) processing layer, and (4) application layer. Subsequently, perception layer focuses on accurate and rapid identification of certain node's information. Network layer is responsible for stability, rapidity, and accuracy of network data transmission rate. Processing layer gathers data of various users' activities, integrate and store them in the system's knowledge base. Concretely, application layer manipulates stored data and invokes inference models to provide results to students through a user-friendly GUI.

Experiments are performed with online real streaming data. Results indicate a well-structured surveillance system proposed to a university campus. A limitation of the adopted research effort is that there are not mentioned the algorithms, which infer an outlier student behavior. Overall it is a robust effort; however, inference algorithms should be presented to be clearer how the system produces a security alarm.

The authors in [98] describe a smart campus surveillance system, which is based on the monitoring of smart buildings, smart classes, smart laboratories, and public spaces. IoT technology exploits Raspberry Pi and sensors capabilities. Passive monitoring is enhanced with RFID, Ethernet, ZigBee, 4G, and LPWAN technologies. Active monitoring is achieved through cameras and microphones installed with university campus infrastructure. A mobile surveillance system design is adopted, which uses cloud-computing potentiality. User context incorporated is based on social, crowdsourcing, and crowd sensing techniques. Software architecture is service-oriented, while inference system is context-aware exploiting AR capabilities. System application is running on mobile environment.

An intrusion detection system is defined, which assures privacy compliance regulations. Security mechanism to face upcoming attacks is based on network monitoring. Acquisition time of research performed is defined, while it is used mixed research methodology. Data context incorporated is based on real sound and video data sources.

Specifically, proposed smart campus unobtrusive monitoring system is based on IoT and AI technologies thus forming an intelligent environment. Such environment is defined as a physical space, which enables innovative and ubiquitous information and communication technologies supporting users to experience and interact with the system's utilities and the generated data sources. Concretely, in such environment students are becoming more active during their interaction with the intelligent smart campus. Subsequently, in this context data generated by IoT devices are able to empower university campus community by providing merged services, which are able to transform the students' daily activities to an advanced well-being experience. Intuitively, collected data sources enable users to participate and interact online and in real time with the intelligent environment. Such interaction is fundamental, since it exploits data visualization methodologies' potentiality enabling other sources of data presentation to the campus community. Adopted system focuses on the creation of a smart campus, which is able to provide students' a variety of intelligent environment's capabilities targeted to the daily needs of the university campus actors. Research exploits the potentiality of a real smart campus, which is characterized by the following aspects, like (1) augmenting the campus with low-cost smart technologies and IoT sensors, (2) deploying smart monitors in public university campus areas to let students interact with the generated data sources as well as being informed about certain contextual phenomena in the spatiotemporal space dimension, and (3) including the potentiality of community users to behave as active participants in exploring and acquire benefits from the intelligent environment and the generated data sources. Proposed system incorporates a specific architecture to support university campus needs. Adopted system architecture is composed of the following layers, such as (1) sensors layer, (2) knowledge base layer, and (3) data visualization layer. Consequently, described layers are supporting effectively the proposed smart campus intelligent system for unobtrusive surveillance safety purposes.

Experimental setup is based in online real sound and video data sources. Results are promising toward a robust surveillance system, which exploits LPWAN capabilities. A limitation of the proposed research effort is that it does not describes the inference algorithms incorporated as well as it does not describe emerged attacks that are treated by the system.

In [99], the authors present a university campus surveillance system, which unobtrusively monitors smart buildings, smart labs, smart parking places, and smart traffic lights. Core IoT technology is based on Arduino Uno, WSN, sensors, and actuators devices. Passive monitoring is able through RFID, GPS, Ethernet, Bluetooth, and LPWAN technologies, while active monitoring is mainly based on cameras and students' smartphones. Surveillance system design is mobile, while computing methodology is based on cloud capabilities. Social, movement and crowdsensing user context is exploited. A big data software architecture is supported, which evaluates unsupervised and semi-supervised inference algorithms potentiality. XR is enhanced with VR techniques, while proposed system is running on mobile platform. Both an authentication and an intrusion detection system are used, which confront with safety and privacy regulations. DoS, eavesdropping, and MTM attacks are faced by adopted anonymization, data encryption, network monitoring, and password security mechanisms. Time span of the effort is mentioned, while research methodology adopted is quantitative. Real data sources are used, which exploit text, image, and video data context.

Specifically, adopted surveillance smart campus safety system focuses on specific campus application areas, security threats, and certain system architectures. Proposed system incorporates IoT security mechanisms, blockchain technology, fog- and edge-computing capabilities, as well as machine learning techniques applied to data generated in distributed environments. Concretely, certain focus is given in the role of machine-to-machine (M2M) connection between IoT devices like sensors and actuators in the university campus. Subsequently, M2M connections cover a broad range of monitoring applications in smart campuses. Intuitively, certain IoT devices are expected to communicate with other devices connected to the internet directly due to IPv6 connectivity. In addition, except of the devices being connected, it is also emerging the concept of social IoT (SIoT), which will enable different social networking students to be connected with the IoT devices where users can share these smart devices over the internet. Such connectivity between IoT applications in university campus emerges the issue of safety and privacy requirements, which can be faced with a trusted and interoperable IoT green ecosystem. Due to these vulnerabilities, adopted IoT applications can create a fertile ground for different kinds of cyber threats, which can be treated with specific security and privacy counter measures. Consequently, IoT application domain is expanding beyond smart campus infrastructure areas, such as being able to be implanted to human body for efficient tacking and security purposes. In addition, such implanting of IoT devices to students' bodies is able to provide effective safety toward cyber-attacks within the university campus where students' act in daily basis. Concretely, in every IoT sustainable ecosystem infrastructure there are specific architectural layers to provide safety to campus population, such as (1) sensors and actuators layer, (2) communication network layer, (3) middleware computation layer, and (4) IoT-enabled end-to-end application layer. All these layers are facing certain compromising problems, which are treated appropriately with certain safety solutions, like (1) blockchain-based solutions, (2) fog computing-based solutions, (3) machine learning solutions, and (4) edge computing-based solutions. Such efficient technical solutions support the unobtrusive operation of the proposed surveillance system.

Experiments are based on text, image, and video real data sources, while results are promising toward an advanced surveillance system for smart campus stability. A limitation of the adopted system is that is does not defines the inference system, which is responsible for deciding the category of an attack that may emerged in the university campus infrastructure.

The researchers in [100] propose a smart campus surveillance system that focuses on smart buildings, public spaces, and smart traffic lights. An IoT platform is incorporated, which exploits Raspberry Pi, Arduino Uno, WSN, sensors, and actuators capabilities. Passive monitoring is based on RFID, Ethernet, Bluetooth, ZigBee, and LPWAN technologies, while active monitoring is achieved by cameras installed on university campus places. Surveillance system design is based on mesh technology, while cloud-computing potentiality is exploited. Social user context is evaluated, while inference system focuses on context-aware principles. Proposed system incorporates supervised learning classification algorithms, while it is running on mobile application environment. Adopted system uses both an authentication and an intrusion detection security system, which confronts with safety and privacy regulations. Certain cryptanalysis, DoS, and jamming attacks are faced by adopted data encryption, biometrics, network monitoring, and firewall security mechanisms. Time acquisition of the efforts is defined, while research methodology used is mixed combining quantitative and qualitative research methods. Data context is based on real and streaming data sources.

Specifically, proposed monitoring university campus safety system is based on a secure IoT sustainable infrastructure able to provide specific countermeasures to face cyberattacks. In addition, the system proposes specific protocols based on certain risk assessment principles to assure privacy and security of the campus. Concretely, contemporary IoT technology represents an optimistic green and sustainable environment. In this environment, IoT devices such as sensors and actuators will be able to utilize internet potentiality and to provide intelligent collaborations between campus population anywhere and anytime. Intuitively, students will be able to use such a system during their daily activity in the university. Such IoT technology is present in a plethora of application fields, such as energy buildings, campus healthcare facilities, as well as green transport within the university. Current research achievements suggest the implementation of a university campus able to support information exchange to students' society, providing advanced services interconnecting physical and digital worlds with certain devices. Concretely, such devices' utilities are based on existing and evolving interoperable information and communication technologies. However, in any communication network, IoT-devices are exposed to various kinds of vulnerabilities and security threats. Subsequently, security is a critical issue for any IoT development. In addition, IoT devices have the ability to interact with their environment automatically and autonomously, which results in a difficult problem while applying security and privacy countermeasures. Consequently, the multiple interconnections between students and devices as well as among IoT devices generate a vast amount of data, which is difficult to manage and further process. Based on these inefficiencies, significant research is performed aiming to examine security issues in the IoT environment, thus being able to determine the safety requirements to be applied to IoT infrastructure. Intuitively, there is a focus on the identification and the application of the security countermeasures required to face upcoming threats and vulnerabilities, which will enable unobtrusive monitoring of university population in a secure smart campus.

Experimental setup focuses on exploitation of real and streaming data sources, while results prove that the proposed research effort university campus surveillance system has efficient behavior in facing emerged malicious attacks. A limitation of the system is that it does not reveal the software architecture it incorporates to perform its effective outcomes.

The authors in [101] present a university campus surveillance system, which examines user unobtrusive monitoring in smart buildings, smart classes, smart labs, smart parking, and smart traffic lights. IoT technology exploits potentiality of WSN, sensors, and actuators. Passive monitoring is achieved through the adoption of RFID, Wi-Fi, 5G, and LPWAN infrastructure, while active monitoring is mainly based on cameras technology. Surveillance system is built upon mobile infrastructure, while it is supported cloud-computing methodology. Adopted system exploits face recognition capabilities, while it is incorporated social and movement user context. Software architecture is based on big data programing design, while inference algorithms adopted include supervised, unsupervised, and semi-supervised model approaches. Proposed system runs on mobile application environment. An intrusion detection system is supported, which confronts with security standards and privacy compliance regulations. Adopted system treats DoS, spoofing, and sniffing malicious attacks with the incorporation of certain anonymization, data encryption, network monitoring, and password security mechanisms. Time span of the effort is mentioned, while research methodology followed is quantitative. Data context contain real, synthetic, streaming, text and image data sources.

Specifically, adopted unobtrusive surveillance smart campus safety system is based on IoT technology enabling network security and intrusion detection mechanisms. Proposed system also exploits the potentiality of machine learning and artificial intelligence (AI) methods and models. Concretely, it is analyzed the Dyn cyberattack, which had exposed the critical fault-lines among smart IoT-enabled networks. Consequently, the danger exposed by such attack compromised not only IoT-connected devices but also threatened the complete internet eco-system in both physical and digital spaces. Intuitively, compromised IoT devices were further used by the cyberattack as botnets to continue compromising their connected devices in a large epidemiological attack scale. Another malware, namely Mirai, was also able to compromise the video surveillance devices resulting in disabling unobtrusive monitoring services of smart campus safety systems. Proposed effort focuses on classifying the observed IoT security threats and proposes solutions to face them as well as protecting surveillance system's infrastructure from other similar attacks in the future. This is able due to an adopted network intrusion detection system (NIDS). Such system is able to sniff network connections and prevent malevolent behavior by untrusted third parties, which are willing to harm smart campus efficiency. NIDS also contains certain knowledge base technology, specific detection security methods, validation strategies, treated threats, and algorithm deployments to face an upcoming cyberattack. In addition, proposed system is able to protect students' activities by incorporating machine learning and AI techniques, which are used to perform detailed students' profiling. Such profiling service is then used to compare a new behavior with an existing one, where if it is observed a certain deviation from normality a security trigger is alarmed. On such alarm, unobtrusive surveillance system takes control to inform security personnel while providing students' a safe environment to prosper.

Experiments are based on real, synthetic, streaming, text, and image data sources, while results indicate that the adopted smart campus surveillance system is robust. A limitation of the system is that it does not analyze in deep detail the inference system it adopts to reach such a stable behavior.

Observed results dictate that there is much work, which should be undertaken. Specifically, in [95], more precise inference algorithms should be incorporated by the adopted surveillance system. Future work is required, in [96], where it should be incorporated in greater detail the user context and the inference algorithms used by the proposed surveillance system. In [97], there is needed more work toward presenting the inference algorithms incorporated to produce an early warning and prevention of an upcoming attack. Future research is required, [98], where it should be mentioned system's inference algorithms and emerged attacks, which is able to face. In [99], more research is needed to be undertaken toward the detailed definition of the inference system, which is supported to secure the proposed system. Further research should be performed, in [100], to reveal and exploit the capabilities of the supported software architecture. In [101], more research work is required to provide in more detail the adopted inference system, which is used to toward such a robust surveillance system behavior.

6

Comparative Assessment

The summary of the comparative assessment performed on this survey is summarized in Table 6.1. Forty-four research efforts, 42 research papers, and 2 patents are reviewed and their strengths and weaknesses are shown. Through the survey, we attempt to classify each system according to our taxonomy developed to depict important parts of the research efforts. Concerning the dimension of physical infrastructure, smart buildings are adopted in 34 systems, smart classes in 10 systems, smart labs in 15 systems, public spaces in 31 systems, smart parking in 8 systems, and smart lighting in 12 systems. Also, smart traffic lights are incorporated in 14 systems, while electric vehicles in 4 systems. Unmanned aerial vehicles (UAV) are used in 3 systems, while connected and autonomous vehicles (CAV) are incorporated only in one system. Regarding the enabling technologies dimension, IoT platform is applied in 35 systems, Raspberry Pi in 7 systems, Arduino Uno in 6 systems, wireless sensor networks (WSN) in 26 systems, sensors in 40 systems, and actuators in 16 systems. Radio frequency identification (RFID) is adopted in 25 systems, global positioning system (GPS) in 23 systems, Ethernet in 12 systems, Wi-Fi in 22 systems, Bluetooth in 17 systems, ZigBee in 10 systems, near-field communication (NFC) in 7 systems, 4G in 5 systems, 5G in 6 systems, and low-power wireless area network (LPWAN) in 7 systems.

Likewise, cameras are incorporated in 37 systems, microphones in 5 systems, smartphones in 18 systems, smart watches in 2 systems, and in automated teller machine (ATM) in 2 systems. Regarding the dimension of software analytics, ad hoc surveillance system design is used in 17 systems, mobile design in 18 systems, and mesh design in 9 systems. Edge-computing methodology is adopted in 4 systems and cloud computing in 23 systems. Voice recognition is incorporated in 2 systems, face recognition in 10 systems, and gesture recognition in 2 systems. Social user context is supported in 21 systems, movement context in 25 systems,

IoT-enabled Unobtrusive Surveillance Systems for Smart Campus Safety,
First Edition. Theodoros Anagnostopoulos.
© 2023 The Institute of Electrical and Electronics Engineers, Inc.
Published 2023 by John Wiley & Sons, Inc.

Table 6.1 Comparative assessment.

Research effort	Physical infrastructure Components/hardware			Enabling technologies Components/hardware				Software analytics Features								System security Components/hardware	System security Features			Research methodology Features	
	Sustainable smart campus	Smart transport	Autonomous vehicles	Core IoT technology	Passive monitoring technology	Active monitoring devices	Surveillance system design	Computing methodology	Affective computing	User context	Software architecture	Inference system	Inference algorithms	XR	Application	Cyber security system	Regulations	Attacks	Security mechanisms	Research context	Data context
[58]	1, 6	2		1, 3, 4, 5, 6	1, 2, 3, 4, 5, 6	1, 3	1					1	1			2	1	7, 10	5, 6, 7	4	1, 3, 5, 8
[59]	2, 4			1, 4, 5	1, 2	3	2	2					1		2	2	1	2, 4	4	1, 2	1, 3, 5
[60]	4, 6			1, 3, 4, 5	2	1, 3	3	2	3	2			1		2	1, 2	1	4	7	2	1, 3, 7
[61]	1, 3, 4			5	2, 4	1, 3	1			1, 2, 3		2	1		2	1, 2	1, 2	6	5, 6, 8	1, 4	2, 4, 8
[62]	3, 4, 5, 6			1, 2, 3, 5, 6	1, 5, 6, 7	1, 2	1	2	2, 3			2			2	2	1	6, 10	3, 6	1, 2	1, 3, 6, 7, 8
[63]	4, 5			1, 5	4	1, 3	2	2		1, 2, 3		2	1		2	1, 2	1	5	7	1, 2	1, 4, 5, 8
[64]	4, 5		1	1, 2, 4, 5	1, 2, 8	1, 2, 3	3	2		1, 2	1	1	1, 2		2	1, 2	2	11	5	1, 2	1, 3, 5, 6, 7, 8
[65]	1, 3, 4, 6	2		1, 2, 3, 4, 5, 6	1, 3, 4, 6, 7	1	1	2		1				1, 2	1, 2	1, 2	2	6	5	2	1, 3, 5
[66]	1, 3, 4, 6	2		1, 4, 5, 6	1, 4	1, 2, 3	1	2	1, 2		1		1		2	1, 2	1		1, 4, 5	1, 3	1, 4, 6, 7, 8
[67]	4		1	1, 4, 5	1, 2	1	1	2			1	2	1, 2		1	1, 2	1, 2	2, 9, 10	1, 3, 4	1, 4	1, 3, 5

[68]	4	1	4, 5	2	1	1	2				2	2	1, 2	1	11	8	2	1, 3, 5
[69]	4	1	5	2, 8, 9	3, 4	2	2		1, 2	1, 2	1	2	2		10	3, 5	1, 2	1, 3, 5
[70]	1, 2		1, 5	1, 2	1	3	2		1			2	2	1	10, 11	6, 8	4	1, 3, 5, 8
[71]	1, 2	1	5	1, 4, 5, 6	1	1	1		2			1	1	1	1	3	2	1, 3, 5
[72]	1, 2		4, 5	4	3	3			2	1		2	1, 2	1, 2	9	1, 3, 5, 7	2	1, 3, 5
[73]	1, 4, 6	1	1	2, 8	1, 3	3		2	2			2	2	1, 2		5	2	1, 4, 8
[74]	1, 4, 6	1	1, 5, 6	1	1	1	1		1, 2, 4	1	2	1, 2	2	1, 2	3	1, 4, 5	1, 4	1, 4, 5, 6, 7, 8
[75]	1, 4, 6	1	1, 4, 5, 6	1, 3, 4, 5, 6	1, 4	3	2	1, 2	1	1, 2	2	2	1	1, 2	1	3, 5	1, 3	1, 3, 5, 7, 8
[76]	1, 3		1, 4, 5	3, 4	3	2	2		2	1, 2	1	2	2			5	1, 3	1, 4, 7
[77]	1, 3		5	1, 5, 7	1, 3	1		2		1	2	1	1, 2	1, 2	10	6, 8	2	1, 3, 5, 7
[78]	1, 3		4	1, 2	1, 3	1			2	1	2	2	2	1	7	4, 5	1, 2	1, 3, 5
[79]	1, 3		1, 2, 5, 6	4	1	1	1	2	1	1, 2, 3	2	2	2	1, 2	7	5	2	1, 3, 7, 8
[80]	1, 4		1, 4, 5, 6	1, 2, 4, 5, 6, 8	1	1	2			1, 3	2	2	2	1, 2		3	1, 2	1, 3, 8
[81]	1, 4		1	2, 4, 5	3	2	2		2	1	1	2	2	1	6	1	2	1, 3, 5
[82]	1, 4		1	1	1	1			1, 2			1, 2	1, 2	2	2, 7, 9	1, 3, 4, 5	1, 3	2, 4, 5
[83]	1, 4		1, 4, 5	1	1	1	2	2	1	1, 3		2	1, 2	1, 2	1, 3, 8	2	2	2, 3, 5, 7
[84]	1, 4		5	2, 9	3	2	2		2, 3, 4	1	2		2	2	5	7	2	1, 3, 5
[85]	1, 4	1	1, 5	1, 2, 4, 5, 7	1, 3	1			1, 2	1	1	2	1, 2	1	6	3, 7	2	1, 4, 7
[86]	1, 4		1, 5	2, 3, 4, 5	3	2			1, 2	1, 2	1	2	1	1	6	4, 5	1, 2	1, 3, 5
[87]	1, 4		1, 4, 5, 6	1, 2, 3, 4, 7, 9	1, 5	3	2		2, 4	1, 2	1	1	1	1, 2		3, 4, 5	2	1, 3, 5, 7, 8
[88]	1, 4	1, 2	1, 4, 5, 6	1, 2, 3, 4, 7, 9	1, 2; 3, 5	3	2		2, 4	1, 2, 3	1	1, 2	1	1, 2		3, 4, 5	2	1, 3, 5, 6, 7, 8
[89]	3, 4		1, 4, 5	1, 3	1	2	2	2	2, 5	1	2	1, 2	2	1		5	1, 4	1, 5, 7, 8
[90]	1, 2, 4, 6		1, 4, 5, 6	2, 4, 5, 6	1, 3	2	2		1, 2, 5	3	1	2	2			1, 5	1, 2	1, 3, 5, 7, 8
[91]	1, 2, 4, 5	2	1, 5	5	1	2	1		1, 5	1	1	2	1	1, 2	2	5	1, 2	1, 3, 8

(Continued)

Table 6.1 (Continued)

Research effort	Physical infrastructure — Components/hardware			Enabling technologies — Components/hardware				Software analytics								System security				Research methodology	
	Sustainable smart campus	Smart transport	Autonomous vehicles	Core IoT technology	Passive monitoring technology	Active monitoring devices	Surveillance system design	Computing methodology	Affective computing	User context	Software architecture	Inference system	Inference algorithms	XR	Application	Cyber security system	Regulations	Attacks	Security mechanisms	Research context	Data context
[92]	1, 3, 4, 6			1, 5	2	1	1	1		1, 4, 5	1	2	1		2	2	1	10	3, 5, 7	1, 4	1, 5
[93]	4	1	1	1, 4, 5	2	1	2	2	2	3, 4, 5	1	2	2, 3	2	1, 2	1	1, 2		5	1, 4	1, 2, 3, 7, 8
[94]	1, 2, 5, 6	1		1, 4, 5	1, 4, 5, 6, 7	1	2	2		4, 5	2	1	1, 2, 3	1	2	1	1	10, 11	5, 8	1, 2	1, 3, 7, 8
[95]	1, 4, 5, 6	2		1, 2, 3, 4, 5, 6	2, 3, 4, 5, 10	1, 3	2	2		1, 2	2	2	1		2	2	1, 2	4	1, 3, 5	1, 3	1, 5, 7, 8
[96]	1, 3	1		1, 4, 5, 6	4, 5, 9, 10	1	2	1			2	2			1, 2	1	1	6	3, 5	1, 2	5, 7
[97]	1, 2, 3			1, 4, 5	1, 2, 5, 9, 10	1	2	2	2	1, 4	1	1			2	1	1, 2		3, 5	1, 4	1, 3, 6, 7, 8
[98]	1, 2, 3, 4			1, 2, 5	1, 3, 6, 8, 10	1, 2	2	2		1, 3, 4	2	1		2	2	2	2		5	1, 4	1, 6, 8
[99]	1, 3, 5	1		1, 3, 4, 5, 6	1, 2, 3, 5, 10	1, 3	2	2		1, 2, 4	1		2, 3	2	2	1, 2	1, 2	2, 3, 7	1, 3, 5, 7	1, 2	1, 5, 7, 8
[100]	1, 4	1		1, 2, 3, 4, 5, 6	1, 3, 5, 6, 10	1	3	2		1	1	1	1		2	1, 2	1, 2	1, 2, 8	3, 4, 5, 6	1, 4	1, 3
[101]	1, 2, 3, 5	1		1, 4, 5, 6	1, 4, 9, 10	1	2	2	2	1, 2	1	1	1, 2, 3	2	2	2	1, 2	2, 5, 6	1, 3, 5, 7	1, 2	1, 2, 3, 5, 7

Legends

Sustainable Smart Campus: (1) Smart Buildings, (2) Smart Class, (3) Smart Labs, (4) Public Spaces, (5) Smart Parking, (6) Smart Lighting

Smart Transport: (1) Smart Traffic Lights, (2) Electric Vehicles

Autonomous Vehicles: (1) Unmanned Aerial Vehicle (UAV), (2) Connected and Autonomous Vehicle (CAV)

Core IoT Technology: (1) IoT Platform, (2) Raspberry Pi, (3) Arduino Uno, (4) Wireless Sensor Networks, (5) Sensors, (6) Actuators

Passive Monitoring Technology: (1) RFID, (2) GPS, (3) Ethernet, (4) Wi-Fi, (5) Bluetooth, (6) ZigBee, (7) NFC, (8) 4G, (9) 5G, (10) Low Power Wide Area Networks (LPWAN)

Active Monitoring Devices: (1) Cameras, (2) Microphones, (3) Smartphones, (4) Smart watches, (5) ATM

Surveillance System Design: (1) Ad hoc, (2) Mobile, (3) Mesh

Computing Methodology: (1) Edge, (2) Cloud

Affective Computing: (1) Voice Recognition, (2) Face Recognition, (3) Gesture Recognition

User Context: (1) Social, (2) Movement, (3) Crowdsourcing, (4) Crowd sensing, (5) Ambient Intelligence (AmI)

Software Architecture: (1) Big Data, (2) Service-oriented

Inference System: (1) Context Aware, (2) Decision Support

Inference Algorithms: (1) Supervised, (2) Unsupervised, (3) Semi supervised

XR: (1) VR, (2) AR

Application: (1) Desktop, (2) Mobile

Cybersecurity System: (1) Authentication System, (2) Intrusion Detection System

Regulations: (1) Security Standards, (2) Privacy Compliance

Attacks: (1) Cryptanalysis, (2) DoS, (3) Eavesdropping, (4) Hacking, (5) Spoofing, (6) Sniffing, (7) Man in the Middle Attack (MTM), (8) Jamming, (9) Data Leakage, (10) Password Capture, (11) Virus Infection

Security Mechanisms: (1) Anonymization, (2) Steganography, (3) Data Encryption, (4) Biometrics, (5) Network Monitoring, (6) Firewall, (7) Password, (8) Antivirus System

Research Context: (1) Acquisition Time, (2) Quantitative, (3) Qualitative, (4) Mixed

Data Context: (1) Real, (2) Synthetic, (3) Streaming, (4) Batch, (5) Text, (6) Sound, (7) Image, (8) Video

crowdsourcing context in 5 systems, crowd sensing context in 10 systems, and AmI in 6 systems. Big data architecture is used in 14 systems, and service-oriented architecture in 9 systems. Context aware system is adopted in 14 systems, and decision support system (DSS) in 16 systems. Supervised machine learning algorithms are incorporated in 32 systems, unsupervised algorithms in 13 systems, and semi-supervised algorithms in 9 systems. Virtual reality (VR) is supported in 4 systems and augmented reality (AR) in 4 systems. Desktop applications are used in 11 systems, while mobile applications in 38 systems.

Regarding the system security dimension, an authentication system is adopted in 24 systems, while intrusion detection systems in 33 systems. Security standards are defined in 36 systems, and privacy compliance in 24 systems. Cryptanalysis attacks are targeted in 4 systems, denial of service (DoS) in 7 systems, eavesdropping in 3 systems, hacking in 3 systems, spoofing in 3 systems, sniffing in 8 systems, man in the middle (MTM) attack in 5 systems, jamming in 2 systems, data leakage in 3 systems, password capture in 8 systems, and virus infection in 4 systems. Anonymization security mechanism is supported in 10 systems, steganography just in 1 system, data encryption in 17 systems, biometrics in 10 systems, network monitoring in 28 systems, firewall in 5 systems, password in 9 systems, and antivirus system in 4 systems. As for the dimension of research methodology, acquisition time of research completion is defined in 28 systems, a quantitative research method in 28 systems, qualitative research method in 5 systems, and a mixed research method in 11 systems. Real data are used in 40 systems, synthetic data in 5 systems, streaming data in 30 systems, batch data in 8 systems, text data in 28 systems, sound data in 7 systems, image data in 22 systems, and video data in 23 systems.

7

Classification and Proposed Solution

Results of current research are mainly focused on the classification of the surveyed research efforts according to the adopted taxonomy, while the final outcome is the proposed solution as a major contribution to the research community. Specifically, classification is based on exploitation of research efforts' significance according to certain metric values. Such metric values are the (1) category normalized weight, (2) normalized values, and (3) values' relative frequencies. The metric values are computed by exhaustively analyzing the context of each effort and depicting its contribution by the proposed taxonomy. Concretely, a weighting process is fundamental to assign quantitative numerical context to the examined metric values. Subsequently, the adopted scoring model is fed with data produced by the weighting process and produces a classification output according to certain values, which divide research efforts to three separate and disjoint classes. Proposed classes are divided based on certain value of adequacy introduced to the scoring model. Each class contains research efforts with similar behavior according to the outcome of the scoring model, while efforts of different classes have dissimilar behavior when compared with efforts of other classes. Based on the inferred three classes according to their efficiency, we propose as a solution the research effort contained in the class with higher adequacy.

7.1 Weighting Process

To perform classification of the surveyed efforts and propose a generic solution, based on the adopted scoring model, we assigned normalized weights, i.e. sum up to 1, on the dimensions, the categories (i.e. components and features), and

IoT-enabled Unobtrusive Surveillance Systems for Smart Campus Safety,
First Edition. Theodoros Anagnostopoulos.
© 2023 The Institute of Electrical and Electronics Engineers, Inc.
Published 2023 by John Wiley & Sons, Inc.

the values of the categories of the proposed taxonomy. The rationale behind the weighing process is to assign higher weights to dimensions, categories, and values of the categories, which have higher impact in IoT-enabled surveillance systems for smart campus, while lower weights are assigned in the opposite case. We assume that dimensions are conceptually regarded as equally weighted, since each dimension emerges a unique niche per surveillance system of the proposed taxonomy. Instead the weights of categories within a certain dimension are varying according to the impact of the category to the surveillance systems. In addition, the values of each category are further weighted to have an in-depth knowledge of the weighting assignment process. Specifically, for the physical infrastructure dimension, we have assigned higher weight to autonomous vehicles category, since it is more challenging to be achieved. Sustainable smart campus follows because buildings are the backbone of the infrastructure, and a smart transport category that has the lowest impact. Inside the autonomous vehicles' component category, unmanned aerial vehicles (UAVs) has higher weight than connected and autonomous vehicles (CAVs), since UAV can record an incident where a CAV cannot reach it. In sustainable smart campus component category, smart buildings have the higher weight, because there are the main places of surveillance in the smart campus, and public spaces, smart parking, smart class, smart labs, and smart lighting follow. In smart transport component category, smart traffic lights achieve higher weight than electric vehicles, because they can capture more incidents, due to their location coverage area. Subsequently, in the enabling technologies dimension, we assigned higher values to active monitoring devices category, because it has higher impact in surveillance process. The core IoT technology category follows, providing technology for surveillance mechanisms. Passive monitoring technology is considered as the passive part of the surveillance process. In the active monitoring devices component category, cameras have the higher weight, because they can capture video and images of individuals in great detail. Microphones follow to provide ambient information, whereas smartphones, smart watches, and automated teller machine (ATM) are used for dedicated purpose only. Within core IoT technology component category, we can distinguish the higher weight of IoT platform, because it processes all data produced from IoT devices, wireless sensor network (WSN), sensors, Arduino Uno, Raspberry Pi follow, which are also have distributed nature and actuators because they perform only reaction processes. Passive monitoring technology component category contains high weights for 4G and 5G communication protocols due to their ambient nature, Wi-Fi, Ethernet, GPS, RFID, Bluetooth, near-field communication (NFC), and ZigBee follow due to their limited coverage area.

Regarding the software analytics dimension, we distinguish high weights for the surveillance system design category, because it is the most significant component in the surveillance process. In descending order of surveillance significance, computing methodology, software architecture, inference system, inference algorithms, user context, affective computing, extended reality (XR), and applications. Specifically, in the surveillance systems design component category, we assign higher weight to a mesh system design because it combines the strengths of other approaches. Ad hoc and mobile system design follow, because they are prone to relocation recording errors. In the computing methodology feature category, we have assigned higher weight to edge computing than to cloud computing, because the edge computing incidents are treated locally and distributed, not overloading the central infrastructure. Next in the software feature category, a higher weight is assigned to the service-oriented architecture than to big data architecture, because emphasis is given to surveillance as a service approach. In the inference system feature category, a higher weight has assigned to context aware system compared with decision support system (DSS), because it achieves an ambient behavior of the system. In addition, in the inference algorithms feature category, we distinguish and apply higher weight to semi-supervised algorithms, because they use advanced machine learning modeling techniques, compared to supervised and unsupervised algorithms. In the user context feature category, we assign higher weight to the movement context, because it enables online location prediction of an abnormal behavior in the campus, compared to crowd sensing, crowdsourcing, and social context. In the affective computing feature category, we assign higher weight to gesture recognition, because it reveals in more detail proactive intention of an individual compared to face and voice recognition. In the XR feature category, we assign higher weight to virtual reality (VR), because it is harder to be implemented in a smart campus environment compared to augmented reality (AR). In the application feature category, we applied higher weight to mobile applications, because they are able to capture more incidents, which are distributed in several locations within the university campus, compared to desktop applications.

Considering the system security dimension, we apply higher weight to cybersecurity system, because it is the core security category compared to the regulations, attacks, and security mechanisms supporting categories. Similarly, in the cybersecurity system component category, we assign higher weight to the authentication system, because it controls the authorized access to the system, compared to the intrusion detection system, which aims at detecting malicious behavior, based on information provided by the authentication system, and forms a second line of defense. In the regulations feature category, the standards have higher weight compared to the privacy compliance, because the standards form the contextual framework of security and privacy. In the attack feature, we assign higher weight to the attacks that happen more frequently, and their descending order from the most frequent to the least one is eavesdropping, sniffing, man in the middle (MTM) attack, data leakage, denial of service (DoS), jamming, virus infection, hacking, password capture, cryptanalysis, and spoofing. In the security mechanisms feature category, we assign higher weight to the countermeasure used more often for system prevention, and their descending order from the most frequent countermeasure to the least frequent one is password, firewall, antivirus system, data encryption, network monitoring, anonymization, steganography, and biometrics. Regarding the research methodology dimension, we assign higher weights for the research context category, because it depicts the research impact of the effort to the scientific community. The data context category used during the research by the effort follows. In the research context feature category, we assigned higher weights in efforts that mention the acquisition time of research completion, because this reveals more information about the work carried out by the researchers. The quantitative research receives higher weight, because its results can be generalized comparing to mixed and qualitative research methods. Subsequently, in the data context feature category, real and streaming data are advanced with higher weights, due to their dynamic nature when compared to batch and synthetic data. In addition, higher weight is assigned to video data, because it is more detailed compared to image, sound, and text data. To further exploit the potential of the adopted scoring model, we also assign normalized relative frequencies, i.e. sum up to 1, to each value of a certain category. Counting and then normalizing the frequency of a specific value that occurs in a certain component or feature category, we produce relative frequencies assignment. Table 7.1 presents an overview of the normalized weights and the relative frequencies for certain dimensions, components, features, and their corresponding values incorporated in the proposed taxonomy.

7.2 Classification Process

Since all taxonomy data has assigned with certain normalized weights and relative frequency values, we feed them to the adopted scoring model to calculate the value of each research effort. Table 7.2 presents the scoring output of all research efforts. Visualization of the scoring percentage for the surveyed research efforts is provided in Figure 7.1.

The final stage of the scoring model is the classification of the research efforts into the three classes. The threshold values v_H and v_M are set by the

Table 7.1 Normalized weights and relative frequencies.

Physical infrastructure	Enabling technologies	Software analytics	System security	Research methodology
		Dimensions' normalized weights are equal to 0.20		
Sustainable smart campus: (1) Smart buildings, (2) smart class, (3) smart labs, (4) public spaces, (5) smart parking, (6) smart lighting	**Core IoT technology:** (1) IoT platform, (2) Raspberry Pi, (3) Arduino Uno, (4) wireless sensor networks, (5) sensors, (6) actuators	**Surveillance system design:** (1) Ad hoc, (2) mobile, (3) mesh	**Cybersecurity system:** (1) Authentication system, (2) intrusion detection system	**Research context:** (1) Acquisition time, (2) quantitative, (3) qualitative, (4) mixed
Category normalized weight: 0.33	**Category normalized weight: 0.33**	**Category normalized weight: 0.20**	**Category normalized weight: 0.40**	**Category normalized weight: 0.67**
Normalized values: (1) 1.00, (2) 0.50, (3) 0.33, (4) 0.83, (5) 0.67, (6) 0.17	**Normalized values:** (1) 1.00, (2) 0.33, (3) 0.50, (4) 0.83, (5) 0.67, (6) 0.17	**Normalized values:** (1) 0.67, (2) 0.33, (3) 1.00	**Normalized values:** (1) 1.00, (2) 0.50	**Normalized values:** (1) 1.00, (2) 0.75, (3) 0.25, (4) 0.50
Values' relative frequencies: (1) 0.31, (2) 0.09, (3) 0.14, (4) 0.28, (5) 0.07, (6) 0.11	**Values' relative frequencies:** (1) 0.29, (2) 0.10, (3) 0.14, (4) 0.24, (5) 0.19, (6) 0.05	**Values' relative frequencies:** (1) 0.39, (2) 0.41, (3) 0.20	**Values' relative frequencies:** (1) 0.42, (2) 0.58	**Values' relative frequencies:** (1) 0.39, (2) 0.39, (3) 0.07, (4) 0.15
Smart transport: (1) Smart traffic lights, (2) electric vehicles	**Passive monitoring technology:** (1) RFID, (2) GPS, (3) Ethernet, (4) Wi-Fi, (5) Bluetooth, (6) ZigBee, (7) NFC, (8) 4G, (9) 5G, (10) low-power wide area networks (LPWANs)	**Computing methodology:** (1) Edge, (2) cloud	**Regulations:** (1) Security standards, (2) privacy compliance	**Data context:** (1) Real, (2) synthetic, (3) streaming, (4) batch, (5) text, (6) sound, (7) image, (8) video
Category normalized weight: 0.17		**Category normalized weight: 0.18**	**Category normalized weight: 0.30**	**Category normalized weight: 0.33**
Normalized values: (1) 1.00, (2) 0.50		**Normalized values:** (1) 1.00, (2) 0.50	**Normalized values:** (1) 1.00, (2) 0.50	
		Values' relative frequencies: (1) 0.18 (2) 0.82	**Values' relative frequencies:** (1) 0.60, (2) 0.40	
		Affective computing: (1) Voice recognition, (2) face recognition, (3) gesture recognition	**Attacks:** (1) Cryptanalysis, (2) DoS, (3) eavesdropping, (4) hacking, (5) spoofing, (6) sniffing, (7) man-in-the-middle attack (MTM), (8) jamming, (9) data leakage, (10) password capture, (11) virus infection	
		Category normalized weight: 0.07		
		Normalized values: (1) 0.14, (2) 0.71, (3) 1.00		
		Values' relative frequencies: (1) 0.14, (2) 0.72, (3) 0.14		
		User context: (1) Social, (2) movement, (3) crowdsourcing, (4) crowd sensing, (5) ambient intelligence (AmI)		
		Category normalized weight: 0.09		
		Normalized values: (1) 0.40, (2) 1.00, (3) 0.60, (4) 0.80, (5) 0.20		

(Continued)

Table 7.1 (Continued)

Physical infrastructure	Enabling technologies	Software analytics	System security	Research methodology
Values' relative frequencies: (1) 0.78, (2) 0.22 **Autonomous vehicles:** (1) Unmanned aerial vehicle (UAV), (2) connected and autonomous vehicle (CAV) **Category normalized weight:** 0.50 **Normalized values:** (1) 1.00, (2) 0.50 **Values' relative frequencies:** (1) 0.75, (2) 0.25	**Category normalized weight:** 0.17 **Normalized values:** (1) 0.50, (2) 0.60, (3) 0.70, (4) 0.80, (5) 0.40, (6) 0.20, (7) 0.30, (8) 1.00, (9) 0.90, (10) 0.10 **Values' relative frequencies:** (1) 0.20, (2) 0.17, (3) 0.09, (4) 0.16, (5) 0.12, (6) 0.07, (7) 0.05, (8) 0.04, (9) 0.05, (10) 0.05 **Active monitoring devices:** (1) Cameras, (2) microphones, (3) smartphones, (4) smart watches, (5) ATM **Category normalized weight:** 0.50 **Normalized values:** (1) 1.00, (2) 0.80, (3) 0.60, (4) 0.40, (5) 0.20 **Values' relative frequencies:** (1) 0.55, (2) 0.07, (3) 0.31, (4) 0.03, (5) 0.03	**Values' relative frequencies:** (1) 0.32, (2) 0.36, (3) 0.08, (4) 0.14, (5) 0.11 **Software architecture:** (1) Big Data, (2) Service-oriented **Category normalized weight:** 0.16 **Normalized values:** (1) 0.50, (2) 1.00 **Values' relative frequencies:** (1) 0.61, (2) 0.39 **Inference system:** (1) context aware, (2) decision support **Category normalized weight:** 0.13 **Normalized values:** (1) 1.00, (2) 0.50 **Values' relative frequencies:** (1) 0.48, (2) 0.52 **Inference algorithms:** (1) Supervised, (2) unsupervised, (3) semi-supervised **Category normalized weight:** 0.11 **Normalized values:** (1) 0.67, (2) 0.33, (3) 1.00 **Values' relative frequencies:** (1) 0.59, (2) 0.24, (3) 0.17 **XR:** (1) VR, (2) AR **Category normalized weight:** 0.04 **Normalized values:** (1) 1.00, (2) 0.50 **Values' relative frequencies:** (1) 0.44, (2) 0.56 **Application:** (1) Desktop, (2) mobile **Category normalized weight:** 0.02 **Normalized values:** (1) 0.50, (2) 1.00 **Values' relative frequencies:** (1) 0.22, (2) 0.78	**Category normalized weight:** 0.20 **Normalized values:** (1) 0.18, (2) 0.64, (3) 1.00, (4) 0.36, (5) 0.09, (6) 0.91, (7) 0.82, (8) 0.55, (9) 0.73, (10) 0.27, (11) 0.45 **Values' relative frequencies:** (1) 0.24, (2) 0.12, (3) 0.05, (4) 0.05, (5) 0.05, (6) 0.14, (7) 0.08, (8) 0.03, (9) 0.05, (10) 0.14, (11) 0.05 **Security mechanisms:** (1) Anonymization, (2) steganography, (3) data Encryption, (4) biometrics, (5) network monitoring, (6) firewall, (7) password, (8) antivirus system **Category normalized weight:** 0.10 **Normalized values:** (1) 0.38, (2) 0.25, (3) 0.63, (4) 0.13, (5) 0.50, (6) 0.88, (7) 1.00, (8) 0.75 **Values' relative frequencies:** (1) 0.11, (2) 0.01, (3) 0.20, (4) 0.11, (5) 0.34, (6) 0.07, (7) 0.10, (8) 0.06	**Normalized values:** (1) 1.00, (2) 0.63, (3) 0.88, (4) 0.75, (5) 0.13, (6) 0.25, (7) 0.38, (8) 0.50 **Values' relative frequencies:** (1) 0.24, (2) 0.03, (3) 0.18, (4) 0.05, (5) 0.18, (6) 0.04, (7) 0.13, (8) 0.14

Table 7.2 Scoring of research efforts.

Research efforts	Score *v*(*i*)	Research efforts	Score *v*(*i*)
[58]	0.399	[80]	0.405
[59]	0.322	[81]	0.322
[60]	0.387	[82]	0.321
[61]	0.333	[83]	0.487
[62]	0.398	[84]	0.285
[63]	0.248	[85]	0.349
[64]	0.267	[86]	0.408
[65]	0.287	[87]	0.380
[66]	0.333	[88]	0.500*
[67]	0.330	[89]	0.346
[68]	0.373	[90]	0.387
[69]	0.253	[91]	0.396
[70]	0.331	[92]	0.330
[71]	0.307	[93]	0.459
[72]	0.287	[94]	0.434
[73]	0.359	[95]	0.398
[74]	0.227	[96]	0.370
[75]	0.400	[97]	0.375
[76]	0.336	[98]	0.318
[77]	0.288	[99]	0.472
[78]	0.411	[100]	0.427
[79]	0.301	[101]	0.438
		[88]	0.500*

* Highest score.

experts and the classified items are shown in Table 7.3. Visualization of the classification percentage for the surveyed research efforts is presented in Figure 7.2.

The proposed solutions are those in the High Adequacy class, namely research efforts [88], [83], [89], [93], [101], [94], [100], [78], [86], and [80], which achieve higher score than the other efforts according to the proposed taxonomy and the adopted scoring model, thus is the outcome of this survey.

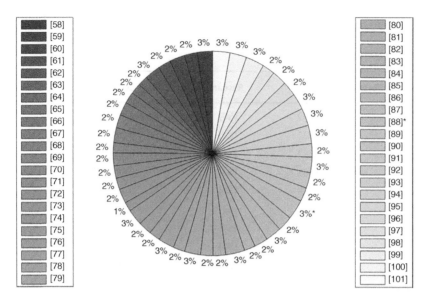

Figure 7.1 Scoring of research efforts visualization.

Table 7.3 Classification of research efforts.

Class	Research effort
High Adequacy ($v_H = 0.405$)	[88], [83], [99], [93], [101], [94], [100], [78], [86], [80]
Medium Adequacy ($v_M = 0.308$)	[75], [58], [62], [95], [91], [60], [90], [87], [97], [68], [96], [73], [85], [89], [76], [61], [66], [70], [67], [92], [59], [81], [82], [98]
Low Adequacy	[71], [79], [77], [65], [72], [84], [64], [69], [63], [74]

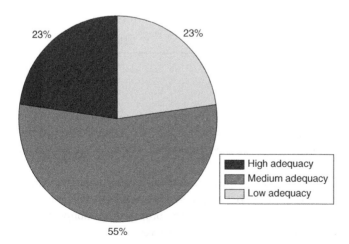

Figure 7.2 Classification of research efforts visualization.

8

Smart Campus Spatiotemporal Authentication Unobtrusive Surveillance System for Smart Campus Safety

A System Architecture

A smart campus spatiotemporal authentication system is proposed, which is based on certain embodiments related to computer software, hardware, networks, and security methods [4, 87, 88]. Such system includes a method of generating a unique identifier for use in authentication process. In particular, embodiments described relate to a unique identifier generated based on a spatiotemporal stochastic history associated with a certain smart campus individual user, like a (1) student, (2) academic, and/or (3) university personnel. Such identifier is denoted as the fingerprint of an individual, which is able to uniquely identify a specific smart campus actor. There exist many scenarios in which campus user authentication is required, for example to provide access to a particular location, to provide access to sensitive information stored on a computing system or to allow a user to perform a particular action, such as to make a bank transfer from an automated teller machine (ATM) located within the smart campus.

Various systems for performing such authentication are proposed in contemporary research [102–104]. For example, quick response (QR) codes have been used extensively for authentication. Concretely, a unique code may be sent to a user's mobile device such as smartphone, smartwatch, smart bracelet, or smart ring, which may be used once to provide authentication for a particular action within the university campus. However, while QR codes are a promising technology for authentication, they do not provide highly scaled safety context awareness of the user's identity. Subsequently, it is not possible to distinguish that a person using the QR code is actually the authorized user to enter the campus. Consequently, if a different person achieves to gain access to the user's mobile device and obtain one of the available QR codes, there would be no way of knowing that the person using the QR code was not the user for whom it was intended.

IoT-enabled Unobtrusive Surveillance Systems for Smart Campus Safety,
First Edition. Theodoros Anagnostopoulos.
© 2023 The Institute of Electrical and Electronics Engineers, Inc.
Published 2023 by John Wiley & Sons, Inc.

One way of providing context awareness of the user's identity is to use acquired spatiotemporal context, which user commonly used on spatial activities upon mapped locations over certain time intervals for few seconds to many years of activity. Such systems, as [103, 104], are examples of an identification system that uses spatiotemporal data sources to identify one single university campus user. Intuitively, in such systems the user's device is used to track patterns in their daily activities. However, a weakness of these systems is that they rely on the fact that the user's device is configured to track their spatiotemporal data, which is activated to do so by the device the user carries during daily engagement within the smart campus.

8.1 Smart Campus Spatiotemporal Authentication Unobtrusive Surveillance System

Smart university campus embodiments incorporated address the emerging weaknesses of contemporary research. Specifically, such embodiments provide a system and method of authentication that uses the spatiotemporal context of a user, which has been measured using third-party monitoring systems. Spatiotemporal data obtained from third-party systems, embodied within the smart campus area, such as closed-circuit television (CCTV) networks, microphone networks, unmanned aerial vehicle (UAV) networks, connected and autonomous vehicle (CAV) networks, electronic pass networks, intelligent surveillance and security robot systems networks [105, 106], as well as humanoid security robots networks [107], are used to determine a spatiotemporal fingerprint that is unique to a university campus individual user. That is, the unique identifier is not derived from a single device carried by the individual, but instead by an amalgamation of data from multiple systems with which the user interacts through the course of daily activity. This fingerprint can then be used to verify a user and detect abnormal and unexpected behavior. Concretely, the individual may be tracked online in real time by a tracking device having global positioning system (GPS) capabilities, such that authorization is granted if the movements of the university actor are in accordance with the spatiotemporal fingerprint of the actor. Conversely, any deviation from the spatiotemporal fingerprint may indicate an intrusion to the smart campus area. For example, the individual may be attempting to access a secure area or asset for which they are not authorized, or a device associated with the individual is in possession of an unauthorized person. Such deviation may then trigger further identification processes to confirm the identity of the individual. Deriving the spatiotemporal fingerprint from third-party data sources eliminates the requirement that the individual is continuously monitored by an implanted device that is set up to measure their spatiotemporal data.

An aspect described provides a computer-implemented method of generating a unique identifier. The method comprises receiving at least one set of sensing data from at least one network of sensing devices arranged to measure the spatiotemporal position of one or more smart campus users, determining from at least one set of sensing data plurality of spatiotemporal data points corresponding to the spatiotemporal position of a user, and generating a unique identifier corresponding to the campus user in dependence on the plurality of spatiotemporal data points. Aspects described may use external sensing systems that are capable of providing multiple data points that indicate the position of a person at various times to generate a unique fingerprint for that person by monitoring the smart campus individual's movements over a certain period of time. Intuitively, systems such as a network of CCTV cameras, a network of microphones, a UAV network, a CAV network, a security robot system network, an interbank network such as an ATM network, a public transport system where a payment card associated with the university user may be used, or card or electronic payment terminals in campus shops, restaurants, or other establishments may be used. In addition, any data collection system where the location of a person is clocked or checked at various times throughout the day for whatever reason can be used to collect a plurality of spatiotemporal data points that can then be used to generate the unique fingerprint that describes the user's usual pattern of activity. Such fingerprint can then be used to verify the identity of the user for authentication purposes. By using external sensing systems that are not located on the user allows a unique identifier to be generated without needing the user to continuously carry a device that is configured to measure their spatiotemporal data.

At least one network of sensing devices may comprise a plurality of sensing devices distributed over a defined geographic area. Subsequently, the network of sensing devices may be a network of CCTV cameras located at various places around a smart campus and connected to face recognition systems to allow a university campus user to be clocked at a particular location at a certain time. To provide more contextual evidence to the proposed smart campus system, it might be considered a set of sensing devices network, which could be a network of microphones located near to the CCTV cameras network. Such network could be connected to voice recognition systems to observe campus user social behavior. In this respect, networks that comprise a dense population of sensing devices over a large geographic area are able to generate a more widespread and detailed unique identifier. In addition, at least one network of sensing devices may comprise at least a first sensing device at a first location and a second sensing device at a second location. Consequently, the first sensing device may be a card reader at an entrance to a first campus transport station, and second sensing device may be a second card reader at an exit to a second campus transport station. Subsequently, another scenario could contain the first sensing device, which could be an ATM machine on a first campus building, while the second sensing device may be a camera on a second campus building. The first university campus user may be repeatedly located at the first and second locations. Concretely, the campus user may be repeatedly located at the first location at a first time on one or more days and repeatedly located at the second location at a second time on one or more days. Subsequently, the first and second campus transport stations may be those visited by the user five days a week on their route to laboratory. Intuitively, the ATM machine may be on the same building as the user's classroom and visited every Monday morning, and the camera may be located on a building on which their laboratory is located such that they pass it every day on their route to laboratory. In some cases, the user may be at the first and the second locations on a periodic basis or it may be that they visit those locations once or twice a week at varying times.

The plurality of spatiotemporal data points determined from at least on set of sensing data may therefore comprise a first set of spatiotemporal data points corresponding to the first location and the first time, and a second set of spatiotemporal data points corresponding to a second location and a second time. The first location may be a first building and the second location be a second building. At least one network of sensing devices is independent of the user. Consequently, the sensing devices are not carried by the user, and there is no requirement that the user activate the sensing devices to measure the spatiotemporal data. Determining at least one set of sensing data to provide plurality of spatiotemporal data points may comprise identifying the user at a plurality of spatiotemporal positions. Such identification may be done in one of many ways depending on the sensing device from which the sensing data came. Intuitively, if a network of sensing devices, such as a network of CCTV cameras incorporates facial recognition software it may be used to identify the user in the CCTV footage. In addition, if the network of sensing devices is a network of microphones, voice recognition software may be used to identify the user in the microphone recordings. Concretely, if a network of sensing devices is an interbank network comprising a plurality of ATM and payment point within the campus or a travel network comprising a plurality of electronic card readers, the user may be identified as the individual associated with a card or other payment device, including mobile devices having electronic wallets, used at one of the devices in those networks. Subsequently, generating the unique identifier may comprise calculating a plurality of vectors having a spatial and temporal component. Collectively, these vectors produce a spatiotemporal map of a student's daily activities in the smart campus. In addition, at least one network of sensing devices is at least one of a group containing (1) a CCTV system, (2) a microphone system, (3) a UAV network, (4) a CAV network, (5) an interbank ATM network, and (6) a network of electronic card or e-payment device readers.

Concretely, receiving at least one set of sensing data may comprise receiving at least one set of sensing data recorded over a predetermined amount of time. Intuitively, the predetermined amount of time may be at least one month, or preferably, at least one year. In this respect, the longer the predetermined time, the more sensing data is collected, and thus the more spatiotemporal data points can be determined for generating the unique identifier. Generally, the more spatiotemporal data points that are used, the more complex the unique identifier is, making it more difficult to imitate the user with which it is associated. Adopted method may further comprise receiving biometric data corresponding to the user and adding the received biometric data to the unique identifier. The biometric data may comprise at least one of the following: (1) facial patterns, (2) gesture patterns, and (3) vocal communication patterns. This adds an additional layer of complexity to the unique identifier, making it even more difficult to imitate. The method may further comprise receiving authorization data corresponding to the user and adding the received authorization data to the unique identifier. Subsequently, the authorization data may comprise information relating to an asset and/or location, wherein the user is authorized to access the asset and/or location. In addition, a second aspect described provides a system comprising a processor and a computer readable medium storing one or more instructions arranged such that when executed the processor is caused to perform the method according to the illustrative smart campus system. Intuitively, a third aspect described provides a method of performing authentication, comprising monitoring the position of a user in dependence on a unique identifier corresponding to the user, wherein the unique identifier is generated to the method of the illustrative university campus system, and verifying the identity of the user if the monitored position matches the unique identifier.

The method of performing authentication may further comprise initiating an identification process if the monitored position is different to the unique identifier. That is, if the monitored position deviates from the expected user's activity defined by the spatiotemporal data points used to generate the unique identifier, formal identification may be required to verify the identity of the user and/or verify that the user is in an authorized location. Concretely, the formal identification process may comprise analyzing one or more video files received from one or more video cameras located in the monitored smart campus area position to verify the identity of the user. Captured video context analyses may be performed using facial and/or gesture recognition software. In addition, the formal identification process could be enhanced by analyzing one or more sound files received from one or more microphones located in the monitored university campus area position to verify the identity of the user. Analyses could be performed using voice recognition software. Intuitively, the method of performing authentication may further comprise activating an alarm, if the identity of the user cannot be verified or if the user is not authorized to be in the monitored position.

8.2 Smart Campus Safety: A System Architecture

An architecture for the adopted system is proposed [88], which provide certain embodiments of spatiotemporal authentication not including biometric context, certain aspects as well as a method of obtaining a unique identifier that can then be used to verify an individual's identity. Such an individual can then be able to get authorized by the system architecture as a person, which has particular purpose such as gain access to a secure location, gain access to sensitive matter, or perform a particular action. System architecture support a method able to provide spatiotemporal authentication not including biometric context is presented in Figure 8.1. Specifically, in Figure 8.1, it is presented that the unique identifier is based on the spatiotemporal history of the smart campus individual, that is their daily activities in the university campus recorded over a prolonged period of time. The spatiotemporal data is collected using third-party monitoring systems (i.e. s.1.2) that are capable of tracking the movements of an individual over a period of time to provide data that records the individual's location, and the time and date that they were at each location. The third-party monitoring systems utilize sensing equipment that is not located on the individual, but rather sensing equipment that is located in a number of geographical locations. That is to say, the sensing devices are independent of the user. Concretely, third-party monitoring system may be a network of CCTV cameras transmitting surveillance footage, which can be processed to identify an individual at a particular location and time. In such cases, facial recognition software may be used to identify the user in the CCTV footage. Spatiotemporal data may also be derived from other third-party

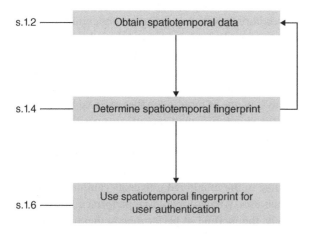

Figure 8.1 Method able to support spatiotemporal authentication not including biometric context.

sources, such as interbank network recording transactions made using a card or other payment device (i.e. a smart phone) associated with the individual. Data received from the interbank network may then be used to derive spatiotemporal data indicating where and when the individual has used their bank card or other payment device. Subsequently, a transport system that uses electronic passes for access and payment, whether the passes be physical card based, or again be embodied within a mobile device provided with radio frequency identification (RFID) style functionality, and capable of emulating a payment or travel card. Intuitively, third-party monitoring systems, which may be used to collect spatiotemporal data, include microphone networks, UAV networks, connected and CAV networks, and surveillance security humanoid robot networks.

Spatiotemporal data can thus be collected based on the smart campus individual's time-stamped location at various times throughout the day as recorded by these external sensing systems. This data may be recorded over several weeks, months, or years to build up a picture of the individual's routine activities to thereby determine a spatiotemporal fingerprint of that individual (i.e. s.1.4). As the spatiotemporal data is recorded over time, patterns will start to emerge in the locations that the individual frequents regularly, as well as the time or day that the individual is usually at those locations. As such an individual may follow the same route from their classroom to the laboratory, twice a day, five days a week, or the individual may visit a particular location within the university campus once a month at a specific time. Therefore, the longer the spatiotemporal data are recorded, the more patterns of activity that emerge and the more detailed the resulting fingerprint, and it will be appreciated that the spatiotemporal fingerprint will evolve over time as more spatiotemporal data are collected. Consequently, the individual may visit a location once every four months. At first, this event may look like an anomaly; however, after several months of recorded spatiotemporal data, it will emerge that this is a pattern of activity that can be written into a fingerprint. As such, a unique spatiotemporal fingerprint is derived that maps the routine day to day movements of the individual while also considering events that occur on a less regular basis but that are still part of the individual's spatiotemporal history. In this respect, the spatiotemporal fingerprint may be a series of spatiotemporal vectors, that is vectors having a spatial and temporal component, describing the user's spatiotemporal context.

In some specific cases, the spatiotemporal fingerprint may also include information relating to high impact areas that the individual may or may not be authorized to enter. In this respect, the high-impact areas may be marked by static or dynamic geofences created to monitor and protect an asset in that area, with the spatiotemporal fingerprint comprising an indication as to whether it is considered normal behavior for that user to cross the geofence. This is particularly useful in security systems monitoring a specific location. Proposed architecture also

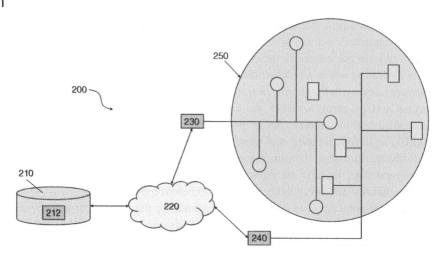

Figure 8.2 Tracking system to provide security in case of attempt to violate a sensitive asset.

supports a tracking system, which is used to provide security in case of attempt to violate a specific location as presented in Figure 8.2. Specifically, a system (i.e. 200) in which a server (i.e. 210) is in communication with third-party servers (i.e. 230, 240) via a network (i.e. 220) is presented. The server (i.e. 210) comprises a processor (i.e. 212) arranged to carry out computing operations. The third-party servers (i.e. 230, 240) are each connected to a network of sensing devices distributed throughout the geographical area of the smart campus (i.e. 250), the sensing devices being capable of collecting data from which spatiotemporal information corresponding to an individual can be derived. Data recorded by each network of sensing devices is collected at the third-party servers (i.e. 230, 240) to extract spatiotemporal data corresponding to an individual and generate a unique fingerprint based on the spatiotemporal data.

Intuitively, it could be the case where one of the third-party servers (i.e. 230) may be that of an interbank network in communication with a plurality of ATM and payment points distributed around the university campus (i.e. 250). Every time an individual completes a transaction using credit or debit card, a data point is recorded comprising a spatial reference corresponding to the location of the ATM or payment point and a time stamp corresponding to the location of the time that the transaction took place. The debit or credit card that recorded that data point can be easily associated with an individual, by means of the name identified on that card. Every time a data point is recorded, it is collected at the third-party server (i.e. 230) and then communicated to the server (i.e. 210) via the network (i.e. 220). The data points already comprise a spatial and temporal component and can therefore be used directly to generate the spatiotemporal fingerprint. The second third-party server (i.e. 240) may then be that of a CCTV system in communication with the plurality of cameras distributed about the smart campus (i.e. 250). Video footage recorded at each of the cameras is transmitted to the CCTV server (i.e. 240) and then communicated to the server (i.e. 210) via the network (i.e. 220). The processor (i.e. 212) will then analyze the video footage to identify the individual, such as using facial recognition software. The video footage is embedded with spatial and temporal metadata; therefore, every time the individual is detected, a spatiotemporal data point can be extracted from the frame in which they are detected, the spatial component corresponding to the location of the camera from which the frame came, and the temporal component corresponding to the time stamp of that frame. Spatiotemporal data corresponding to an individual can thus be collected from the interbank server (i.e. 230) and the CCTV server (i.e. 240) to generate a spatiotemporal fingerprint for that individual. Consequently, the system (i.e. 200) comprises a plurality of sensing devices located at different locations within the geographic area of the university campus (i.e. 250), such as the sensing devices may be located in several classrooms and on several laboratories within the geographical area of smart campus (i.e. 250). Spatiotemporal data is then collected from the sensing devices at locations that the campus individual visits repeatedly. In addition, it could be possible that the individual may repeatedly visit a first university campus building around the same time on one or more days a week, and similarly visit a second university building at another time on one or more days a week. As such, the spatiotemporal data collected for that individual comprises a series of data points corresponding to the first and the second campus buildings and the times at which those buildings are visited. Subsequently, the third-party servers (i.e. 230, 240) may be connected to any sensing devices capable of recording a time-stamped spatial reference that can be associated with the individual.

In some cases, the spatiotemporal fingerprint may also be supplemented with additional biometric data. Specifically, such a method able to provide spatiotemporal authentication including biometric context is presented in Figure 8.3. Concretely, biometric data may be obtained from analysis of a network of cameras and microphones (i.e. s.3.2), from which the individual's facial patterns, gesture patterns, and vocal communication patterns can be determined. This biometric data can then be added to the spatiotemporal fingerprint of the individual (i.e. s.3.4). This can be particularly useful in providing a further way to identify the individual in authorization systems. Subsequently, consider a system where video footage is collected from a network of CCTV cameras, the video footage may be analyzed further to derive biometric data for the university individual in addition to the spatiotemporal data sources. Once the spatiotemporal fingerprint has been determined, the spatiotemporal fingerprint may be used as part of an authorization system.

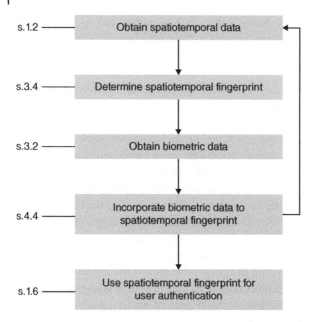

Figure 8.3 The method able to support spatiotemporal authentication including biometric context.

Consequently, a method of authentication that uses the spatiotemporal fingerprint to verify the identity of a smart campus individual and to anticipate unauthorized behavior is also possible with the collected data from the university campus. Such authentication method, which is based on spatiotemporal context, is presented in Figure 8.4. To monitor a particular area or location in the smart campus, individuals within the monitored area may be tracked (i.e. s.4.4), by using the GPS capability of a mobile device associated with the individual. In this respect, the spatial context of an individual is expressed as an actual geographic coordinate or as a relational coordinate of a predefined location in an infrastructure, thereby the spatial context being time-stamped to monitor the spatiotemporal trajectory of that individual (i.e. s.4.4). If the individual crosses a geofence of a high-impact area or requests access to a secure location or asset, the spatiotemporal trajectory is compared to the spatiotemporal fingerprint of the individual to determine whether that individual is deviating from their normal behavior (i.e. s.4.6), by crossing a geofence that they are not authorized to cross or significantly deviate from the normal pattern of activity. If the trajectory has bot deviated from the spatiotemporal fingerprint, that is the movements of the individual are as expected, no alarm is triggered and the individual is authorized to access the area or asset (i.e. s.4.8). If the trajectory of the individual has deviated from

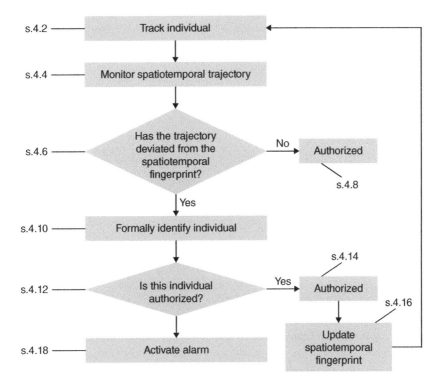

Figure 8.4 Authentication method based on spatiotemporal context.

spatiotemporal fingerprint, an early warning is triggered and a request to formally identify the individual is initiated (i.e. s.4.10). Various methods may be employed to try to formally identify the individual, such as video and/or audio files may be obtained from a CCTV system operating in the location of the individual. Facial and/or vocal recognition software may then be employed to analyze the video and/or audio files to determine the identity of the individual (i.e. s.4.12). If, upon identification, the individual is known and considered to be authorized for access to that area or asset (i.e. s.4.14), the early warning can be deactivated and authorization of the individual confirmed. This may be the case, where the individual has only been authorized for a particular area or asset, and is consequently not yet part of the individual's spatiotemporal fingerprint. In such cases, new spatiotemporal data may be derived from this deviation in expected activity and used to update the spatiotemporal fingerprint for that individual (i.e. s.4.16). If the individual cannot be identified, or alternatively, the individual can be identified but is not authorized for access to the area or asset, an alarm may be activated (i.e. s.4.18) to prompt further action.

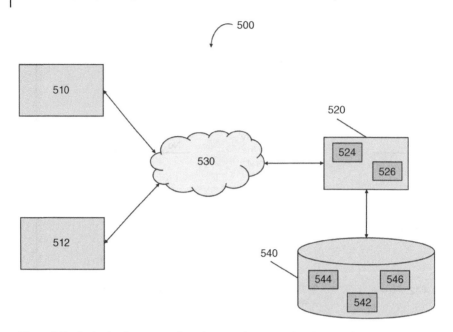

Figure 8.5 Authorization system based on spatiotemporal authentication method.

An authorization system, which can address the emerging technical issues of the adopted authentication method, may be used. Specifically, such a proposed authorization system is presented in Figure 8.5. Concretely, it is defined a smart campus system (i.e. 500) comprises a server (i.e. 520) in communication with third-party servers (i.e. 510, 512) via a network (i.e. 530) through a communication interface (i.e. 524). The server (i.e. 520) comprises a processor (i.e. 526) arranged to carry out computing operations and is also in communication with a core server (i.e. 540). The core server (i.e. 540) runs different software-implemented modules that carry out different tasks or provide particular data when required by the processor (i.e. 526). More specifically, a spatiotemporal fingerprint module (i.e. 542) is arranged to calculate and store the spatiotemporal fingerprint, while a spatiotemporal trajectory module (i.e. 544) is arranged to track the spatiotemporal of individuals within an area to be monitored in dependence on the spatiotemporal fingerprints. The core server (i.e. 540) also comprises an authorization module (i.e. 546) arranged to perform formal identification of any individuals that have a spatiotemporal trajectory deviating from the normal and authorized behavior provided for in the spatiotemporal fingerprint.

Intuitively, the server (i.e. 520) is arranged to receive data via network (i.e. 530) from the third-party servers (i.e. 510, 512), from which spatiotemporal data for input to the adjacency module (i.e. 544) can be extracted. This data may include any form of information from which the location of an individual can be tracked. The server (i.e. 520) may also be arranged to receive instructions from a third-party server (i.e. 510, 512) relating to one or more individuals for which a spatiotemporal fingerprint is to be generated. These instructions may also provide details of the area that is monitored, including any geofences for specific high-impact areas, and an indication of which individuals are authorized to enter the high-impact areas and which individuals are not. Data and instructions received from the third-party servers (i.e. 510, 512) are communicated to the core server (i.e. 540), which inputs the data to the spatiotemporal module (i.e. 542). The spatiotemporal module (i.e. 542) then extracts spatial and temporal data relating to an individual identified in the instructions and uses this to generate a spatiotemporal fingerprint. The spatiotemporal trajectory module (i.e. 544) is then arranged to track one or more individuals in the area to be monitored as described above based on spatiotemporal fingerprints extracted from the spatiotemporal fingerprint module (i.e. 542). When an individual cross a geofence or requests access to an area or asset within the area being monitored, the spatiotemporal trajectory module (i.e. 544) compares the individual's movements to their spatiotemporal fingerprint to determine whether the individual has deviated therefrom. If the individual has deviated from the spatiotemporal fingerprint, the spatiotemporal trajectory module (i.e. 544) will send an alert to the authorization module (i.e. 546), which prompts the authorization module (i.e. 546) to carry out formal identification of the individual. If the authorization module (i.e. 546) detects an unauthorized individual, an alarm is then communicated to the server (i.e. 520) to signal to the user that further action may be required. If the authorization module (i.e. 546) verifies that the individual is authorized, the authorization model (i.e. 546) will communicate this information to the spatiotemporal fingerprint module (i.e., 542), which will then update the spatiotemporal fingerprint for that individual.

An example in use of the authorization system (i.e. 500) will be described. The server (i.e. 520) may receive instructions from a certain first third-party server (i.e. 510) via network (i.e. 530) The first third-party server (i.e. 510) may be that of university campus wanting to monitor the whereabouts of smart campus individuals moving around a campus building that comprises restricted areas and/or assets, such as particular files stored in a computer system. The instructions may be therefore include a list of university users authorized to enter the building, details regarding the restricted assets and/or areas, and the university personnel who are authorized to access each of those restricted assets and/or areas. Concretely, to calculate spatiotemporal fingerprints for each of the university users, the server (i.e. 520) may then request data from another second third-party server (i.e. 512). The second third-party server (i.e. 512) may be a CCTV provider, the data being video files relating to a network of CCTV cameras installed in a particular geographic area within the campus. In this respect, the geographic area might be a single building or an area of land, such as public spaces of smart campus. Subsequently, a geographic area might be the building to be monitored, with CCTV cameras being located in one or more classrooms of the building or include the whole area of the smart campus in which the building is located with CCTV cameras being located in a number of other buildings within the university campus. Consequently, the instructions received from the first third-party server (i.e. 510) and the data received from the second third-party server (i.e. 512) will then be communicated to the core server (i.e. 540), which inputs the instructions and the data to the spatiotemporal fingerprint model (i.e. 542) for analysis. For each individual identified in the instructions, the spatiotemporal fingerprint module (i.e. 542) will analyze their movements as included to the CCTV footage to determine patterns of activity that can be added to their spatiotemporal fingerprint. Intuitively, to achieve this, the spatiotemporal fingerprint module (i.e. 542) will implement some suitable means of identifying each individual in the footage, such as using facial recognition software. As well as series of spatiotemporal vectors described their daily activities, the resulting spatiotemporal fingerprint may also include information relating to the areas and assets for which the individual has authorized access and/or areas and assets for which the individual does not have authorized access.

Subsequently, once the spatiotemporal fingerprints for the required smart campus users have been determined, the spatiotemporal trajectory module (i.e. 544) will monitor the movements of the university campus users in dependence on the spatiotemporal fingerprints. In this respect, the spatiotemporal trajectory of the campus users may be tracked using suitable means, such as the GPS capability of a device associated with an individual, CCTV cameras, or electronic security passes used to open doors within a campus building. Concretely, the spatiotemporal trajectory module (i.e. 544) will track the movements of the individual, and if that individual crosses a geofence or requests access to an area or asset, the spatiotemporal module (i.e. 544) will compare the individual's movements to their spatiotemporal fingerprint. If the spatiotemporal trajectory matches the spatiotemporal fingerprint, the individual is authorized and provided with the necessary access. If the trajectory has deviated from the spatiotemporal fingerprint, such as by crossing a geofence into an area that they are not authorized to be, an alert is triggered and communicated to the authorization module (i.e. 546). Intuitively, the authorization module (i.e. 546) will then initiate formal identification of the individual. Consequently, the authorization module (i.e. 546) may send a request to the server (i.e. 520) for real-time CCTV footage from the second third-party server (i.e. 512) in the location where the unauthorized individual has been detected. On receipt of the relevant CCTV video files, the authorization module (i.e. 546) will analyze the video files to identify the individual, by manual inspection or using facial recognition software. If the individual cannot be identified as recognized university campus user or is identified as a campus user not authorized for access to that particular area and/or asset, the authorization module (i.e. 546) will send alert to the server (i.e. 520), triggering an alarm. In the presented example, the spatiotemporal fingerprint module (i.e. 542), the spatiotemporal trajectory module (i.e. 544), and the authorization module (i.e. 546) are proposed to be implemented on the same processor and core server. However, in practice it could be suggested that each of these modules may be implemented on separate distributed systems, such as the spatiotemporal fingerprints may be generated separately and distributed to a third party for use in the authentication system.

9

Human Factor as an Unobtrusive Surveillance System's Adoption Parameter for Smart Campus Safety

As far as now, the concept of smart campus along with its possible malicious attacks by third-party individuals, which aim to cause harm either to infrastructure and/or to university campus users, is presented. An analysis on the kind of threats a smart campus is possible to suffer is performed and certain countermeasures are proposed, which secure the campus system from unauthorized behavior. However, such a protection from malevolent individuals raises issues of privacy sacrifices to assure a safety working place for the campus users. Ethical dilemma is appeared, which has to be treated rationally to make feasible the adoption of a monitoring system by academics, students, and university personnel. In addition, there arises an issue relevant to the degree of engagement with such a safety system by campus population, since users in general wish to be secured by malicious third parties but also not sharing their personal data with the system. Such concern is going to emerge the issue of trust to the unobtrusive surveillance campus system. In the adopted system, a negotiation schema is proposed, which aims to face trust issues between the monitoring system and the user free will to engage with it in a viable manner.

9.1 Ethical Dilemma of Adopting an Unobtrusive Surveillance System

Preservation of university campus safety from malevolent third-party individuals is a principle, which is presented in detail in this research effort. Concretely, there arise certain ethical dilemmas that are useful to be taken into consideration by policy makers and other stakeholders when designing a sustainable green

IoT-enabled Unobtrusive Surveillance Systems for Smart Campus Safety,
First Edition. Theodoros Anagnostopoulos.
© 2023 The Institute of Electrical and Electronics Engineers, Inc.
Published 2023 by John Wiley & Sons, Inc.

surveillance system. Certain issues should be considered, such as (1) privacy, (2) ethical, and (3) social implications of a monitoring smart campus system. Authors in [108] proposed a system that faces ethics and security constrains based on a methodology for constructing several slightly different but closely related methods, which focuses on ethical dilemma scenarios. Subsequently, it becomes clear that when designing a safety campus system, ethical dilemma scenario is not immediately apparent. This is the reason that forces policy makers to undertake a privacy and ethical impact assessment as well as engaging stakeholders in the process to identify and analyze the upcoming social issues. In addition, further studies in the area of agent-based social simulation (ABSS) in relation to the study of social dilemmas such as the Prisoner's Dilemma (PD) and Tragedy of the Commons (TC) are used to explain the ethical dilemma of accepting a smart campus surveillance system for providing safety services to campus users [109]. Specifically, ABSS research can focus on the deep understanding of social phenomena by using synthetic data produced in environments of crowed human daily activity. Such analysis is able to explain certain behaviors like human population's choice to undertake the ethical dilemma of accepting university monitoring for social well-being in a smart campus. Emergence of unobtrusive surveillance safety smart campus systems would not be applicable without significant progress in the area of cyber security AI. In [110, 111] there are presented the reasons, which make artificial intelligence (AI) able to overcome the ethical dilemmas of adoption in a plethora of smart systems. Research concludes that attempting to change the world of advanced technology is feasible only when a set of reasons are present, such as (1) technical maturity, (2) human understanding, (3) policy makers elasticity, and (3) willingness to collaborate all of the actors together to achieve the creation of a social aware and safe smart campus environment.

9.2 Degree of Free Will Engagement and Negotiation with an Unobtrusive System

In the adopted smart campus unobtrusive safety system [88], a certain architecture to be evaluated by interested policy makers and stakeholders is proposed. Such system architecture deals with smart campus safety and privacy issues. However, the final decision whether such a smart campus architecture is going to be adopted by university individuals and used in practice is an open issue. Such a decision should be able to address certain ethical dilemmas emerged by the incorporation of the system in real world. Humans are subjects, which are characterized by high degree of free will in any conceptual or applicable action they perform during their life. Actually, the whole civilization is based on the respect of humans' free will to do and act the way they prefer whenever and wherever they judge they would like to. The key principle behind such behavior is the right of each individual to be a free person with a unique personality, which requires respect from the other persons and/or entire civilized world. The only case where such freedom is suppressed is when the actor performs certain malevolent behavior. That is, in case of small fault, the person is being advised not to commit a minor offense again. However, in case of a defect, the person is advised not to violate again. In addition, there are cases where the actor does not remorse and then it is highly possible to be sentenced until it complies with the acceptable behavior of the rest of the human population. Concretely, in the later cases privacy of an individual is suspend due to delinquent behavior and this is in comply with human laws. Intuitively, the adoption of the proposed system by the user requires user's consent to store and handle their private data and information for further analytical processing by the monitoring system. Actually, safety could only be assured in case campus users' give consent to provide access to the system to store their private data. This is exactly the problem that such kind of safety systems suffer to be adopted by humanity.

The proposed solution is feasible to be incorporated by university campus users by providing them the option to negotiate their degree of free will and freedom with the safety system. That is providing the end users the feasibility to share their private data with the system in the degree they wish to enjoy unobtrusive surveillance system's safety services. This negotiation between the user and the system is possible to be implemented with several levels of membership loyalty. Such levels might start with the entry level to the system that is giving consent to use actor's spatiotemporal data to enter and move within the system with limited access to system's services. It could be certain intermediate levels of membership loyalty where might provide more access to users by invoking their distinguished levels of provided biometric context to feed the system providing secure access levels to more places in the university campus. Consequently, it would also be feasible that a physical entity gives whole consent to the system to use their private data. In such a case, the user could be characterized as full membership loyalty member who will enjoy all systems services. However, there is another issue to be emerged that is the degree these actors are enjoying safety services by the adopted system. Intuitively, according to the level of membership loyalty scenario, it will be provided high safety to full members, adequate security services to intermediate-level members, and limited safety services to entrance-level members. This is exactly the notion of a member to negotiate the degree of engagement with the system, that is the system can protect any of its members in the degree of free will the member trusts the proposed unobtrusive surveillance safety smart campus system.

10

Smart Campus Surveillance Systems Future Trends and Directions

In this book, an analytical survey was performed on internet of things (IoT)-enabled smart campus surveillance systems available in the literature. This book is focused on smart campus as a socially acceptable solution, since contemporary universities are open to change management as well as to experiment intuitively with unknown safety situations. Specifically, there are some real implications, which make these systems acceptable by the scientific community, such as prevent and repression of a delinquent behavior as well as studying the motivation and the development behind this behavior. Such knowledge will be of high importance when designing and evaluating advanced surveillance systems in smart cities, like the one in London, UK, to prevent terrorism and terrorist attacks. Proposed survey is based on certain dimensions derived from the surveyed papers and patents, following certain conceptual patterns. The motivation behind this survey is that only relevant surveillance systems will be examined having a trace to all dimensions, which are (1) smart campus physical infrastructure, (2) IoT core enabling technologies, (3) predictive software analytics, (4) system security and management, and (5) applied research methodology. A scoring model designed to evaluate the proposed taxonomy is adopted. The outcome of the survey is a classification of the research efforts, providing a set of proposed research efforts to be further analyzed by the scientific community and industry, according to their utility toward surveillance systems. The findings of this survey, conducted to reveal crucial security relevance and other issues, are valuable and applicable for the construction of any robust surveillance model designed specifically for smart campuses.

This construction should incorporate modules with advanced technological achievements that will efficiently supervise and monitor a modern smart campus system, toward preventing its uninterruptible operation and improving the

IoT-enabled Unobtrusive Surveillance Systems for Smart Campus Safety,
First Edition. Theodoros Anagnostopoulos.
© 2023 The Institute of Electrical and Electronics Engineers, Inc.
Published 2023 by John Wiley & Sons, Inc.

standards of the provided services. Important aspects in this future research direction should be the proposed taxonomy and the results produced by the classification process. The survey findings have showed the five main dimensions defined for the taxonomy, the physical infrastructure, the enabling technologies, the software analytics, the system security, and the research methodology, should be incorporated as discrete key features and will formulate independent modules in surveillance systems for smart campuses. In addition, the derived findings of the weighted scoring model, proposed in the adopted taxonomy, might be exploited to construct a secure architecture for efficient smart campus surveillance systems. Intuitively, we could further expand the results of the current survey in the future to consider patents that will be produced by the surveyed research papers, while start-ups that will emerge based on the surveyed patents will also be analyzed. The aim of our future work is to research the impact of scientific invention in the area of IoT-enabled smart campus surveillance systems to industrial innovation for mankind well-being. Concretely, it is obvious that the main issues of the adoption of such unobtrusive surveillance systems by humanity is not the technical advancements but rather the ethical dilemmas arise in the new era of digitized social monitoring. Lessons learnt throughout this study indicate that monitoring systems should be applied in adult university campus population only in case there are supportive techniques, which may be able to protect privacy of university campus actors. Finally, such systems should provide the university users the ability to decide in what depth may the users wish to interact with the surveillance infrastructure while simultaneously not to get their private data exposed to delinquent third parties.

References

1 Hernandez, M.A.R., Sacristan, A.G., and Cuadrado, D.G. (2019). SimulCity: planning communications in smart cities. *IEEE Access* 7: 46870–46884.

2 Hidalgo, C.G., Hortelano, D., Sanchez, L.R. et al. (2018). IoT heterogeneous mesh network deployment for human-in-the-loop challenges towards a social and sustainable industry 4.0. *IEEE Access* 6: 28417–28437.

3 Cheng, B., Zhu, D., Zhao, S., and Chen, J. (2016). Situation-aware IoT service coordination using the event-driven SOA paradigm. *IEEE Transactions on Network and Service Management* 13 (2): 349–361.

4 Anagnostopoulos, T., Kostakos, P., Zaslavsky, A. et al. (2021). Challenges and solutions of surveillance systems in IoT-enabled smart campus: a survey. *IEEE Access* 9: 131926–131954.

5 Kirimtat, A., Krejcar, O., Kertez, A., and Tasgetiren, M.F. (2020). Future trends and current state of smart city concepts: a survey. *IEEE Access* 8: 86448–86467.

6 Sharif, R.A. and Pokharel, S. (2022). Smart city dimensions and associated risks: review of literature. *Sustainable Cities and Society* 77: 1–14.

7 Apostol, D., Balaceanu, C., and Constantinescu, E.M. (2015). Smart – economy concept – facts and perspectives. *Journal of Business and Public Administration* 6 (3): 67–77.

8 Nilssen, M. (2018). To the smart city and beyond? Developing a typology of smart urban innovation. *Technological Forecasting and Social Change* 142: 98–104.

9 Ismagilova, E., Huges, L., Dwivedi, Y.K., and Raman, K.R. (2018). Smart cities: advances in research – an information systems persepective. *International Journal of Information Management* 47: 88–100.

10 Paiva, S., Ahad, M.A., Tripathi, G. et al. (2021). Enabling technologies for urban smart mobility: recent trends, opportunities and challenges. *Sensors* 21 (6): 1–45.

IoT-enabled Unobtrusive Surveillance Systems for Smart Campus Safety,
First Edition. Theodoros Anagnostopoulos.
© 2023 The Institute of Electrical and Electronics Engineers, Inc.
Published 2023 by John Wiley & Sons, Inc.

11 Radu, L.D. (2020). Disruptive technologies in smart cities: a survey on current trends and challenges. *Smart Cities* 3 (3): 1022–1038.

12 Appio, F.P., Lima, M., and Paroutis, S. (2018). Understanding smart cities: ionnovation ecosystems, technical advancements, and societal challenges. *Technological Forecasting and Social Change* 142: 1–14.

13 Coelho, V.N., Oliveira, T.A., Tavares, W., and Coelho, I.M. (2021). Smart accounts for decentralizing governance on smart cities. *Smart Cities* 4 (2): 881–893.

14 Ahad, M.A., Paiva, S., Tripathi, G., and Feroz, N. (2020). Enabling technologies and sustainable smart cities. *Sustainable Cities and Society* 61: 1–42.

15 Sharma, A., Podoplelova, E., Shapovalov, G. et al. (2021). Sustainable smart cities: convergence of artificial intelligence and blockchain. *Sustainability* 13: 1–13.

16 Sossou, A.M.E., Galvez, D., Deck, O. et al. (2020). Sustainable risk management strategy selection using a fuzzy multi-criteria decision approach. *International Journal of Disaster Risk Reduction* 45: 1–15.

17 Alghamdi, A. and Shetty, S. (2016). Survey toward a smart campus using the internet of things. *Proceedings of the IEEE FiCloud*, Vienna, Austria, pp. 235–239.

18 Allah, N.M. and Alrashed, S. (2020). Smart campus – a sketch. *Sustainable Cities and Society* 59: 1–15.

19 Ahmed, A., Ahmad, A., Piccialli, F. et al. (2017). A robust features-based person tracker for overhead views in industrial environment. *IEEE Internet of Things Journal* 5 (3): 1598–1605.

20 Bibri, S.E. and Krogstie, J. (2017). Smart sustainable cities of the future: an extensive interdisciplinary literature review. *Sustainable Cities and Society* 31: 183–212.

21 Fortes, S., Ramon, J.A.S., Palacios, D. et al. (2019). The campus as a smart city: University of Malaga environmental, learning, and research approaches. *Sensors* 19 (6): 1–23.

22 Huang, L.S., Su, J.Y., and Pao, T.L. (2019). A context aware smart classroom architecture for smart campuses. *Applied Sciences* 9 (9): 1–34.

23 Kolokotsa, D., Gobakis, K., Papantoniou, S. et al. (2016). Development of a web based energy management system for University Campuses: the CAMP-IT platform. *Energy and Buildings* 123 (1): 119–135.

24 Nagarajan, S.G., Zhang, P., and Nevat, I. (2017). Geo-spatial location estimation for internet of things (IoT) networks with one-way time-of-arrival via stochastic censoring. *IEEE Internet of Things Journal* 4 (1): 205–214.

25 Livaja, I., Skvorc, D., and Pripuzic, K. (2017). Geospatial publish/subscribe systems for the internet of things. *Proceedings of the IEEE SoftCOM*, Split, Croatia, pp. 1–8.

26 Cao, X. and Mardia, S. (2019). Efficient geospatial data collection in IoT networks for mobile edge computing. *Proceedings of the IEEE NCA*, Cambridge, MA, pp. 1–10.

27 Lwin, K.K., Sekimoto, Y., Takeuchi, W., and Zettsu, K. (2019). City geospatial dashboard: IoT and big data analytics for geospatial solutions provider in disaster management. *Proceedings of the Proceedings of the IEEE ICT-DM*, Paris, France, pp. 1–4.

28 Zhang, J., Wang, Y., Li, S., and Shi, S. (2021). An architecture for IoT-enabled smart transportation security system: a geospatial approach. *IEEE Internet of Things Journal* 8 (8): 6205–6213.

29 Kamilaris, A. and Ostermann, F.O. (2018). Geospatial analysis and the internet of things. *International Journal of Geo-Information* 7 (269): 1–22.

30 Rieke, M., Bigagli, L., Herle, S. et al. (2018). Geospatial IoT – the need for event-driven architectures in contemporary spatial data infrastructures. *International Journal of Geo-Information* 7 (385): 1–29.

31 Kang, L. (2020). Street architecture landscape design based on wireless internet of things and GIS system. *Microprocessors and Microsystems* 80 (103362): 1–7.

32 Miloudi, L. and Rezeg, K. (2019). Leveraging the power of integrated solutions of IoT and GIS. *Proceedings of the IEEE PAIS*, Tebessa, Algeria, pp. 1–7.

33 Mena, M., Corral, A., Iribarne, L., and Criado, J. (2019). A progressive web application based on microservices, combining geospatial data and the internet of things. *IEEE Access* 7: 104577–104590.

34 Wang, L., Yao, C., Yang, Y., and Yu, X. (2018). Research on a dynamic virus propagation model to improve smart campus security. *IEEE Access* 6: 20663–20672.

35 Mullins, J. (2006). Ring of steel II – New York City gets set to replicate London's high-security zone. *IEEE Spectrum* 43 (7): 12–13.

36 Storck, C.R. and Duarte-Figueiredo, F. (2020). A survey of 5G technology evolution, standards, and infrastructure associated with vehicle-to-everything communications by internet of vehicles. *IEEE Access* 8: 117593–117614.

37 Zourmand, A., Hing, A.L.K., Gung, C.W., and Rehman, M.A. (2019). Internet of Things (IoT) using LoRa technology. *Proceedings of the IEEE I2CACIS*, Selangor, Malaysia, pp. 324–330.

38 Iqbal, M., Abdullah, A.Y.M., and Shabnam, F. (2020). An application based comparative study of LPWAN technologies for IoT environment. *Proceedings of the IEEE TENSYMP*, Dhaka, Bangladesh, pp. 1857–1860.

39 Dian, F.J. and Vahidnia, R. (2020). LTE IoT technology enhancements and case studies. *IEEE Consumer Electronics Magazine* 9 (6): 49–56.

40 Elgarhy, O., Reggiani, L., Malik, H. et al. (2021). Rate-latency optimization for NB-IoT with adaptive resource unit configuration in uplink transmission. *IEEE Systems Journal* 15 (1): 265–276.

41 Chishti, M.S., King, C.T., and Banerjee, A. (2021). Exploring half-dublex communication of NFC read/write mode for secure multi-factor authentication. *IEEE Access* 9: 6344–6357.

42 Lavric, A., Petrariu, A.I., and Popa, V. (2019). Long range SigFox communication protocol scalability analysis under large-scale high-density conditions. *IEEE Access* 7: 35816–35825.

43 Long, S. and Miao, F. (2019). Research on ZigBee wireless communication technology and its application. *Proceedings of the IEEE IAEAC*, Chengdu, China, pp. 1830–1834.

44 Galeano-Brajones, J., Garmona-Murillo, J., Valenzuela-Valdes, J.F., and Luna-Valero, F. (2020). Detection and mitigation of DoS and DDoS attacks in IoT-based stateful SDN: an experimental approach. *Sensors* 20 (816): 1–18.

45 Liao, C.H., Shuai, H.H., and Wang, L.C. (2018). Eavesdropping prevention for heterogeneous Internet of Things systems. *Proceedings of the IEEE CCNC*, Las Vegas, NV, pp. 1–2.

46 Wang, N., Jiao, L., Wang, P. et al. (2018). Efficient identity spoofing attack detection for IoT in mm-wave and massive MIMO 5G communication. *Proceedings of the IEEE GLOBECOM*, Abu Dhabi, United Arab Emirates, pp. 1–6.

47 Ahmad, F., Adnane, A., Franqueira, V.N.L. et al. (2018). Man-in-the-middle attacks in vehicular ad-hoc networks: evaluating the impact of attackers' strategies. *Sensors* 18 (4040): 1–19.

48 Shin, S.H. and Kobara, K. (2016). A secure anonymous password-based authentication protocol with control of authentication numbers. *Proceedings of the IEEE ISITA*, Monterey, CA, pp. 325–329.

49 Carracedo, J.M., Milliken, M., Chouhan, P.K. et al. (2018). Cryptography for security in IoT. *Proceedings of the IEEE IoTSMS*, Valencia, Spain, pp. 23–30.

50 Khraisat, A., Gondal, I., Vamplew, P., and Kamruzzaman, J. (2019). Survey of intrusion detection systems: techniques, datasets and challenges. *Cybersecurity* 2 (20): 1–22.

51 Lei, H., Wang, D., Park, K.H. et al. (2020). Safeguarding UAV IoT communication systems against randomly located eavesdroppers. *IEEE Internets of Things Journal* 7 (2): 1230–1244.

52 Keeney, R.L. and Raiffa, H. (1993). *Decisions with Multiple Objectives – Preferences and Value Tradeoffs*, 1–569. Cambridge, NY: Cambridge University Press.

53 Siskos, E. and Tsotsolas, N. (2015). Elicitation of criteria importance weights through the Simos method: a robustness concern. *European Journal of Operational Research* 246 (2): 543–553.

54 Figueira, J. and Roy, B. (2001). Determining the weights of criteria in the ELECTRE type methods with a revised Simos' procedure. *European Journal of Operational Research* 139: 317–326.

55 Pictet, J. and Bollinger, D. (2008). Extended use of the cards procedure as a simple elicitation technique for MAVT. Application to public procurement in Switzerland. *European Journal of Operational Research* 185 (3): 1300–1307.

56 Solymosi, T. and Dombi, J. (1986). A method for determining the weights of criteria: the centralized weights. *European Journal of Operational Research* 26 (1): 35–41.

57 Tsotsolas, N., Spyridakos, A., Siskos, E., and Salmon, I. (2019). Criteria weights assessment through prioritizations (WAP) using linear programming techniques and visualizations. *Operational Research International Journal* 19: 135–150.

58 Datta, S. and Sarkar, S. (2017). Automation, security and surveillance for a smart city: smart, digital city. *Proceedings of the IEEE CALCON*, Kolkata, India, pp. 26–30.

59 Chang, Y.C. (2012). Evaluation and exploration of optimal deployment for RFID services in smart campus framework. In: *Computer Science and Its Applications. Lecture Notes in Electrical Engineering*, vol. 203 (ed. S.S. Yeo, Y. Lee and H. Chang), 493–502. Dordrecht, Netherlands: Springer.

60 Gahlaut, S. and Seeja, K.R. (2017). IoT based smart campus. *Proceedings of the IEEE ICICCI*, Grater Noida, India, pp. 1–4.

61 Sun, G., Zhou, Y., and Li, J. (2016). Building smart campus using human behavioral data. *Proceedings of the IEEE UIC-ATC-ScalCom-CBDCom-IoP-SmartWorld*, Toulouse, France, pp. 133–136.

62 Rao, M., Neetha, R., Swathi, M. et al. (2018). An IoT based smart campus system. *International Journal of Scientific & Engineering Research* 9 (4): 146–151.

63 Huang, Y., White, C., Xia, H., and Wang, Y. (2017). A computational cognitive modeling approach to understand and design mobile crowdsourcing for campus safety reporting. *International Journal of Human – Computer Studies* 102 (C): 27–40.

64 Abdullah, A., Thanoon, M., and Alsulami, A. (2019). Toward a smart campus using IoT: framework for safety and security system on a university campus. *Advances in Science, Technology and Engineering Systems Journal (ASTESJ)* 4 (5): 97–103.

65 Phougat, K., Sinha, M., Pruthi, S., and Wakurdekar, S.B. (2017). An IoT approach for developing a smart campus. *International Journal of Innovative Research in Computer and Communication Engineering* 5 (4): 7405–7412.

66 Uskov, V.L., Bakken, J.P., Karri, S. et al. (2018). Smart university: conceptual modeling and systems design. In: *Smart Universities, International Conference on Smart Education and Smart E-Learning (SEEL), Smart Innovation, Systems, and Technologies*, vol. 70 (ed. V. Uskov, J. Bakken, R. Howlett and L. Jain), 49–86. Cham, Switzerland: Springer.

67 Wang, L., Li, K., and Chen, X. (2018). Internet of things security analysis of smart campus. In: *International Conference on Cloud Computing and Security (ICCCS), Lecture Notes in Computer Science*, vol. 11067 (ed. X. Sun, Z. Pan and E. Bertino), 418–428. Cham, Switzerland: Springer.

68 Sarker, K.U., Daraman, A.B., Hasan, R. et al. (2019). Kids' smart campus ontology to retrieve interest. *Proceedings of the IEEE MEC-ICBDSC*, Muscat, Oman, pp. 1–4.

69 Concone, F., Ferraro, P., and Re, G.L. (2018). Towards a smart campus through participatory sensing. *Proceedings of the IEEE SMARTCOMP*, Taormina, Italy, pp. 393–398.

70 Gao, B., Liu, F., Du, S., and Meng, F. (2018). An OAuth2.0-based unified authentication system for secure services in the smart campus environment. In: *Computational Science, International Conference on Computational Science (ICCS), Lecture Notes in Computer Science*, vol. 10862 (ed. Y. Shi et al.), 752–764. Cham, Switzerland: Springer.

71 Rehman, A.U., Abbasi, A.Z., and Shaikh, Z.A. (2008). Building a smart university using RFID technology. *Proceedings of the IEEE ICCSSE*, Hubei, China, pp. 641–644.

72 Zhang, L., Oksuz, O., Nazaryan, L. et al. (2016). Encrypting wireless network traces to protect user privacy: a case study for smart campus. *Proceedings of the IEEE WiMob*, New York, pp. 1–8.

73 Ferreira, J.E., Visintin, J.A., Okamoto, J., and Pu, C. (2017). Smart services: a case study on smarter public safety by mobile app for University of Sao Paulo. *Proceedings of the IEEE SmartWorld-SCALCOM-UIC-ATC-CBDCom-IOP-SCI*, San Francisco, CA, pp. 1–5.

74 Ch, W.V., Pacheco, X.P., and Mora, S.L. (2019). Application of a smart city model to a traditional university campus with a big data architecture: a sustainable smart campus. *Sustainability* 11 (2857): 1–28.

75 Arshad, S., Azam, M.A., Ahmed, S.H., and Loo, J. (2017). Towards information-centric networking (ICN) naming for internet of things (IoT): the case of smart campus. *Proceedings of the ACM ICFNDS*, Cambridge, United Kingdom, pp. 1–6.

76 Tian, Z., Cui, Y., An, L. et al. (2018). A real-time correlation of host-level events in cyber range service for smart campus. *IEEE Access* 6: 35355–35364.

77 Beqqal, M.E., Kasmi, M.A., and Azizi, M. (2016). Access control system in campus combining RFID and biometric based smart card technologies. In: *Europe and MENA Cooperation Advances in Information and Communication Technologies, Advances in Intelligent Systems and Computing*, vol. 520 (ed. A. Rocha, M. Serrhini and C. Felgueiras), 559–569. Cham, Switzerland: Springer.

78 Pinggui, H. and Xiuqing, C. (2017). Design and impementation of campus security system based on internet of things. *Proceedings of the IEEE ICRIS*, Huai'an, China, pp. 86–89.

79 Nikouei, S.Y., Chen, Y., Song, S. et al. (2018). Smart surveillance as an edge network service: from Harr-Cascade, SVM to a lightweight CNN. *Proceedings of the IEEE ICCIC*, Philadelphia, PA, pp. 256–265.

80 Chen, L.W., Chen, T.P., Chen, D.E. et al. (2018). Smart campus care and guiding with dedicated video footprinting through internet of things technologies. *IEEE Access* 6: 43956–43966.

81 Liu, K., Warade, N., Pai, T., and Gupta, K. (2017). Location-aware smart campus security application. *Proceedings of the IEEE SmartWorld-SCALCOM-UIC-ATC-CBDCom-IOP-SCI*, San Francisco, CA, pp. 1–8.

82 Zheng, L., Song, C., Cao, N. et al. (2018). A new mutual authentication protocol in mobile RFID for smart campus. *IEEE Access* 6: 60996–61005.

83 Popescu, D.E., Prada, M.F., Donescu, A. et al. (2018). A secure confident cloud computing architecture solution for a smart campus. *Proceedings of the IEEE ICCCC*, Oradea, Romania, pp. 240–245.

84 Alimpertis, E., Markopoulou, A., Butts, C., and Psounis, K. (2019). City-wide signal strength maps: prediction with random forests. *Proceedings of the ACM WWW*, San Francisco, CA, pp. 2536–2542.

85 Goel, D., Kher, E., Joag, S. et al. (2010). Context-aware authentication framework. In: *Mobile Computing, Applications, and Services, (MobiCASE), Lecture Notes of the Institute for Computer Sciences, Social Informatics and Telecommunications Engineering*, vol. 35 (ed. T. Phan, R. Montanari and P. Zerfos), 16–41. Heidelberg, Berlin, Germany: Springer.

86 Yu, Z., Liang, Y., Xu, B., et al. (2011). Towards a smart campus with mobile social networking. *Proceedings of the IEEE ICIoT-ICCPSC*, Dalian, China, pp. 162–169.

87 Anagnostopoulos, T. (2021). Spatiotemporal authentication. European Patent 3,407,232 B1.

88 Anagnostopoulos, T. (2020). Spatiotemporal authentication. US Patent 10,824,713 B2.

89 Bazhenov, N. and Korzun, D. (2019). Event-driven video services for monitoring in edge-centric internet of things environments. *Proceedings of the IEEE FRUCT*, Helsinki, Finland, pp. 47–56.

90 Korzun, D., Balandina, E., Kashevnik, A. et al. (2019). Ambient intelligence services in IoT environments: emerging research and opportunities. *IGI Global* 1–199.

91 Hassani, A., Medvedev, A., Haghighi, P.D. et al. (2018). Context-as-a-service platform: exchange and share context in an IoT ecosystem. *Proceedings of the IEEE PerCom*, Athens, Greece, pp. 385–390.

92 Bates, O. and Friday, A. (2017). Beyond data in the smart city: repurposing existing campus IoT. *IEEE Pervasive Computing* 16 (2): 54–60.

93 Rimboux, A., Dupre, R., Dacu, E. et al. (2019). Smart IoT cameras for crowd analysis based on augmentation for automatic pedestrian detection, simulation and annotation. *Proceedings of the IEEE DCOSS*, Santorini, Greece, pp. 304–311.

94 Chang, Y.C. and Lai, Y.H. (2020). Campus edge computing network based on IoT street lighting nodes. *IEEE Systems Journal* 14 (1): 164–171.

95 Alvarez-Campana, M., Lopez, G., Vazquez, E. et al. (2017). Smart CEI moncloa: am IoT-based platform for people flow and environmental monitoring on a smart university campus. *Sensors* 17 (2856): 1–24.

96 Kulkarni, P., Hakim, Q.O.A., and Lakas, A. (2020). Experimental evaluation of a campus-deployed IoT network using LoRa. *IEEE Sensors Journal* 20 (5): 2803–2811.

97 Xu, X., Li, D., Sun, M. et al. (2019). Research on key technologies of smart campus teaching platform based on 5G network. *IEEE Access* 7: 20664–20675.

98 Prandi, C., Monti, L., Ceccarini, C., and Salomoni, P. (2019). Smart campus: fostering the community awareness through an intelligent environment. *Mobile Networks and Applications* 25: 945–952.

99 Hassija, V., Chamola, V., Saxena, V. et al. (2019). A survey on IoT security: application areas, security: application areas, security threats, and solution architectures. *IEEE Access* 7: 82721–82741.

100 Radoglou-Grammatikis, P.I., Sarigiannidis, P.G., and Moscholios, I.D. (2018). Securing the internet of things: challenges, threats and solutions. *Internet of Things* 5: 41–70.

101 Chaabouni, N., Mosbah, M., Zemmari, A. et al. (2019). Network intrusion detection for IoT Security based on learning techniques. *IEEE Communications Surveys & Tutorials* 21 (3): 2671–2701.

102 Anagnostopoulos, T. (2014). A surveillance system for preventing suicide attempts in urban metro stations. *Proceedings of the ACM PCI*, Athens, Greece, pp. 1–6.

103 Albayram, Y., Kentros, S., Jiang, R., and Bamis, A. (2013). A method for improving mobile authentication using human spatio-temporal behavior. *Proceedings of the IEEE ISCC*, Split, Croatia, pp. 305–311.

104 Lima, J.C.D., Rocha, C.C., Augustin, I., and Dantas, M.A.R. (2011). A context-aware recommendation system to behavioral based authntication in mobile and pervasive environments. *Proceedings of the* IEEE IFIP, Melbourne, VIC, Australia, pp. 312–319.

105 Kim, K., Bae, S., and Huh, K. (2010). Intelligent surveillance and security robot systems. *Proceedings of the IEEE ARSO*, Seoul, South Korea, pp. 1–4.

106 Salh, T.A. and Nayef, M.Z. (2013). Intelligent surveillance robot. *Proceedings of the IEEE ICECCPCE*, Mosul, Iraq, pp. 1–6.

107 Trovato, G., Lopez, A., Paredes, R., and Cuellar, F. (2017). Security and guidance: two roles for a humanoid robot in an interaction experiment. *Proceedings of the IEEE RO-MAN*, Lisbon, Portugal, pp. 230–235.

108 Wright, D., Finn, R., Gellert, R. et al. Ethical dilemma scenarios and emerging technologies. *Technological Forecasting & Social Change* 87: 325–336.

109 Gotts, N.M., Polhill, J.G., and Law, A.N.R. Agent-based simulation in the study of social dilemmas. *Artificial Intelligence Review* 19: 3–92.

110 Saetra, H.S., Coeckelbergh, M., and Danaher, J. (2021). The AI ethicist's dilemma: fighting Big Tech by supporting Big Tech. *AI and Ethics* https://doi.org/10.1007/s43681-021-00123-7.

111 Strumke, I., Slavkovik, M., and Madai, V.I. (2021). The social dilemma in artificial development and why have to solve it. *AI and Ethics* https://doi.org/10.1007/s43681-021-00120-w.

Index

IoT-enabled Unobtrusive Surveillance Systems for Smart Campus Safety,
First Edition. Theodoros Anagnostopoulos.
© 2023 The Institute of Electrical and Electronics Engineers, Inc.
Published 2023 by John Wiley & Sons, Inc.

Printed and bound by CPI Group (UK) Ltd, Croydon, CR0 4YY

27/10/2024

14580672-0004